INDEX

GW01471498

ABOUT THIS BOOK

This is a revision book, not a text book. It will show you everything you need to know in the Math Studies syllabus, but it assumes that you have already covered the work, and that you are now going through it for the second (or third, or fourth ....) time. I would expect you to use your other resources (text book, class notes) to fill in much of the detail.

The exam is not so much a test of your knowledge and understanding (you will not get a question which begins "What do you know about ....?"); but a test of how you use your understanding to solve mathematical problems. So the emphasis in this revision book is on how to answer questions. In particular you will find plenty of worked exam style questions, as well as further ones for *you* to solve. All the questions in boxes are of a standard and of a type that could occur in your exams. Do not skim over these – much useful revision material is contained in the working which is not contained in the text.

You are expected to be able to understand and use your graphic display calculator (GDC) in many areas of the syllabus. Indeed, some questions *require* you to use, for example, the graphing or the equation solving features. Since different people use different calculators, it is not possible for this book to explain the detail of their use; but I have indicated (using the calculator symbol 🖩) where the GDC can be particularly useful. If you have a calculator from the TI-83 family, you might like to know that another book in the OSC Revision Guide series, "Using the TI-83 calculator in IB Maths", will guide you through all the techniques you need.

This is *your* revision book. Every page has a wide column for you to make notes and scribblings and write down questions to ask your teacher; the "You Solve" questions generally have enough space for you to write down your own working. And on the next page there are some important points about how to maximise your exam mark. *Do* follow the suggestions there, and perhaps add some more of your own.

At the very end there are some practice questions testing you on the basic work contained in each area of the syllabus.

Through Oxford Study Courses I have been privileged to help many students revise towards their IB Mathematics exams, and much of what I have learnt from teaching them has been distilled into this book. I would value any feedback so that later editions can continue to help students around the world. Please feel free to e-mail me on inlucas@greentrees.fsnet.co.uk. All correspondence will be answered personally.

Ian Lucas

MAXIMISING YOUR MARKS

Remember that the examiner is on your side – he *wants* to give you marks! Make it easy for him to find them, even if you are not quite sure what you are doing or if you are getting wrong answers. You cannot *lose* marks for doing things wrong. LEARN THIS CHECKLIST.

Before you start a question:
- Read it carefully so you know what it is about.
- Highlight important words.

Answering a question:
- Check any calculations you do, preferably using a different method or order of operation.
- Show your working – there are often marks for method as well as for the right answer. And, in a longer question, a wrong answer at the start may mean lots more wrong answers – but the examiner will probably give you marks for correct methods, and will check your working against your original answer.
- Make sure you have answered *exactly* what the question asked. For example, have you been asked to calculate the new value of an investment or the amount of interest earned.
- In longer questions, don't worry if you can't work out the answer to a part. Carry on with the rest, using their answer (if one is given) or even making up a reasonable answer.
- Don't spend too long on any question or part of a question – you may lose the opportunity to answer easier questions later on. You can always come back and fill in gaps.
- The algebra can be tough – keep going!
- Check the units in questions – are they mixed?

The "golden three":
- WHAT are you working out?
- HOW are you going to work it out?
- WHAT is the answer?

eg: Where do the lines
$y = x + 3$ and $x + 2y = 0$
intersect?

Lines intersect when $y = -2y + 3$
$$3y = 3$$
$$y = 1$$
Point of intersection = $(-2, 1)$

| WHAT | HOW | ANSWER |

Diagrams:
- Do not assume facts from diagrams, especially if they are marked NOT TO SCALE. For example, it may *look* like a right angle but does the question *tell* you that it is. Two lines may *look* parallel but they aren't unless you are *told* they are.
- And do draw your own diagrams – not necessarily to hand in as part of the question, but to help you sort out what's going on.

Key words in questions:
- STATE – put the answer down without working (should be an easy one)!
- WRITE DOWN – minimal working required.
- SHOW – show enough working to get to the given answer.
- EVALUATE – give a value to, work out.
- SKETCH A GRAPH – draw its shape and show key points (eg: where it cuts the axes)
- PLOT A GRAPH – work out points and draw the graph accurately
- EXACT VALUE – not a rounded decimal eg: 2π, not 6.28...

SHOW $x = 3$ is the solution of
$2x + 1 = 7$.
$$2 \times 3 + 1 = 7$$
(We have not had to *solve* the equation)

When you have answered the question:
- Check you have answered every part of the question.
- Check you have answered exactly what was asked.
- Check you have answered to the correct accuracy (normally 3 SF)
- Check that what you have written is clear, and that your answer is not mixed up in the working somewhere.

DO THESE CHECKS – you will probably pick up a few marks.

NUMBER AND ALGEBRA

Number Systems and Accuracy

Different situations require different types of number. For example, populations of countries will always be given as positive, whole numbers, whereas the division of a reward will require the use of fractions. These are known as *number systems*, and the ones you need to know are:

Natural numbers – positive whole numbers
Integers – whole numbers including negatives and zero
Rationals – numbers which can be written as fractions in their simplest form
Irrationals – numbers which can't be written as fractions
Reals – the rationals and the irrationals put together. The reals will include every possible number you could meet in the course.

Decimals do not seem to feature in the list above – are they rational or irrational?

Recurring decimals can always be written as fractions so they are rational numbers.
Terminating decimals can also be written as fractions, so they are rational numbers too.
Non-recurring, non-terminating decimals (ie they carry on for ever and never repeat) can never be written as an exact fraction, so they are irrational numbers.

Exact values: $\sqrt{4} = 2$ since 4 is a square number. However, $\sqrt{10}$ cannot be written exactly – nor can the majority of square roots. It is 3.16228... (the dots indicate that the decimal places will continue for ever without recurring). To 4 significant figures, $\sqrt{10}$ is 3.162, but what do you do if the question asks for an *exact* value? The answer is to use the square root notation:
$$x^2 = 10 \Rightarrow x = \sqrt{10}$$
and this is the only exact way to write down the solution. And, especially if this is an intermediate answer to a question, it is often better for calculation purposes.

To be strictly accurate, $x = \pm\sqrt{10}$

eg: Find the lengths *a* and *b*.

$a^2 = 9^2 + 4^2 = 97 \Rightarrow a = \sqrt{97}$
$b^2 = a^2 - 5^2 = 97 - 25 = 72$

So $b = \sqrt{72}$. The calculation would have been longer (and possibly less accurate) if we had worked out $\sqrt{97}$ as a decimal and used that.

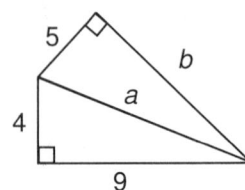

Accuracy: When answering questions which have numerical solutions, it is important to understand how to round numbers to an appropriate level of accuracy. If there are 6 people in a room, then 6 is perfectly accurate. However, a length given as 6cm implies that it lies between 5.5cm and 6.5cm. Strictly, the 6.5 would actually be rounded to 7, so we could say: $5.5 \leq 6 < 6.5$

Note that the number 6.0 implies a greater accuracy:

$$5.95 \leq 6.0 < 6.05$$

You should not give *all* the figures on your calculator because it is possible to be *too* accurate. Consider the following: what is the area of a rectangle with dimensions 4.2cm by 3.8cm? Because the dimensions cannot be accurate (no measurement ever is) the numbers 4.2 and 3.8 represent the ranges shown in the diagram. So the *least* possible value of the area is $4.15 \times 3.75 = 15.5625$ and the *greatest* value of the area is $4.25 \times 3.85 = 16.3625$. In other words:

$$15.5625 \leq area < 16.3625$$

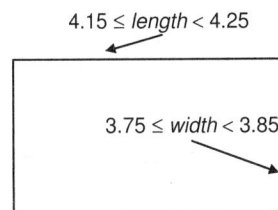

$4.15 \leq length < 4.25$

$3.75 \leq width < 3.85$

If we had worked out the area as $4.2 \times 3.8 = 15.96cm^2$ this just would not be true – it is too accurate. In general, answers should not contain more figures of accuracy than the original numbers – in this case, we would say that area $\approx 16cm^2$. As a *general* rule, you can't go too far wrong if you give answers to 3 significant figures.

Significant figures and decimal places: Consider the number 4127. Altering the 4 to a 5 has much more effect on the number than altering the 7 to an 8 – we say that the 4 (ie the number of thousands) is the *most significant* digit. The first significant figure is the first non-zero digit, and the digits which follow (including zeroes) are the 2nd, 3rd, 4th significant figures, and so on. When rounding to, say, 3 significant figures (shortened to S.F.) we write down the first three significant digits, rounding the 3rd up if the 4th is at least 5. It may be necessary to fill spaces with zeroes.

Examples of rounding to 3 S.F:

$16.836 \approx 16.8$
$251.93 \approx 252$
$0.01315 \approx 0.0132$
$23465 \approx 23500$
$12.961 \approx 13.0$ *(The 0 here is significant)*

Note that the decimal point has no effect on the rounding process. However, when rounding to, say, 3 decimal places (D.P.) we simply count up the figures after the decimal point – and then round in exactly the same way.

Examples of rounding to 2 D.P:

$2.1445 \approx 2.14$
$131.131 \approx 131.13$
$0.0291 \approx 0.03$
$1.2951 \approx 1.30$

Rounding errors: In some questions, you may have to do several calculations to get to the answer. You should try and keep all the figures on your calculator as you work and only round the *final* answer to the required accuracy. Otherwise, rounding errors will accumulate and your answer could be some way out. This is especially true when powers are involved. Work out $\sqrt{15}$ on your calculator, then raise it to the power 5. If you were to round $\sqrt{15}$ to 3.9, and then raise it to the power 5, just see the difference it makes to the answer!

Percentage error: No measurements are completely accurate; it is important to know how significant any errors are. The best way to express errors is as a percentage of the measurement. For example, I can measure a line to the nearest 0.5cm – what is the percentage error when measuring a line which is 14cm long?

The actual error (0.5cm) is called the *absolute error*
0.5 is 3.6% of 14 – this is the *percentage error*

Use your calculator to find the percentage error when the fraction 22/7 is used to approximate the value of π.
(Hint: Don't forget that your calculator has a π button).

YOU SOLVE

<u>0.04%</u>

Reminder about percentages:
You should be able to do the following types of calculation:

Answers:
2.856
15.3%
2205
15.624
$285.71

What is 12% of 23.8?
What is 56 as a percentage of 365?
Increase 2100 by 5%.
Decrease 18.6 by 16%.
A coat costs $300 including 5% sales tax. What is the cost of the coat before tax?

Estimation: Estimation is an important mathematical ability. Estimating the answer to a problem (especially a practical problem) doesn't mean that you are unable to work out the accurate answer – only that you want to have a *rough* idea of the size of the answer. How long will it take me to fly from Berlin to Rome? It's about 1500km and planes fly at about 800km/h, so the flying time is just under 2 hours – that's an estimate. The actual distance is 1537km, and the plane I am in is actually flying at 825km/h – this gives the flight time as 1.86 hours.

When asked to calculate an estimate, round the numbers to 1 S.F. and you should find the calculation fairly easy to do.

For example, an estimate for $\dfrac{3.8^2 \times 2.1}{7.8}$ is $\dfrac{4^2 \times 2}{8} = 4$ To 3 S.F., the correct answer is 3.89.

You are also expected to be able to assess whether your answers to questions are reasonable, and this requires the application of common sense as well as estimates. Which of the following answers to questions do you think require a rethink?

The height of the building is 2.7m
The area of the triangle is $-6cm^2$
The car was travelling at 68 km/h
The mean weight of an egg is 34kg
He ran 200m in 25 seconds

Standard Form

The exponential expression a^b: You must understand the meaning of negative and fractional powers as well as positive, whole number powers. Let's look at powers of 2:

Powers up here have the conventional meaning of multiplying a number by itself several times. $\longrightarrow$	$2^4 = 16$
	$2^3 = 8$
	$2^2 = 4$

a^1 is always a for all values of a a^0 is always 1 for all values of a $\longrightarrow$	$2^1 = 2$
	$2^0 = 1$

Negative powers *never* make the number itself negative. A negative power means "take the reciprocal". So, $a^{-n} = \dfrac{1}{a^n}$ $\longrightarrow$	$2^{-1} = \frac{1}{2} = \frac{1}{2^1}$
	$2^{-2} = \frac{1}{4} = \frac{1}{2^2}$
	$2^{-3} = \frac{1}{8} = \frac{1}{2^3}$

Fractional powers always involve *roots*. The power $\frac{1}{2}$ means the square root, the power $\frac{1}{3}$ means the cube root; the power $\frac{3}{2}$ means the cube of the square root. These can be combined with a negative sign to give, for example:

$$3^{-\frac{2}{5}} = \frac{1}{(\sqrt[5]{3})^2}$$

In general, $a^{\frac{1}{n}} = \sqrt[n]{a}$ and $a^{\frac{m}{n}} = \left(\sqrt[n]{a}\right)^m = \sqrt[n]{a^m}$

Examples:
$2.5^1 = 2.5$

$4^{-2} = \dfrac{1}{16}$

$\left(\dfrac{2}{3}\right)^{-3} = \left(\dfrac{3^3}{2^3}\right) = \dfrac{27}{8}$

$8^{\frac{5}{3}} = \left(\sqrt[3]{8}\right)^5 = 32$

Standard form: Standard (or scientific) form gives us a way of writing very large and very small numbers without using lots of zeroes. eg:

$$43000 = 4.3 \times 10000 = 4.3 \times 10^4$$
$$23\,000\,000 = 2.3 \times 10\,000\,000 = 2.3 \times 10^7$$
$$0.00056 = 5.6 \times \frac{1}{10000} = 5.6 \times 10^{-4}$$
$$0.000000109 = 1.09 \times \frac{1}{10000000} = 1.09 \times 10^{-7}$$

It is important that the first part of the number is between 1 and 10. If you do a calculation and the answer comes out as 12×10^4 this is not in standard form: it must be written as 1.2×10^5.

- A common mistake is to write eg 4.1×10^3 as 4.1^3
- 🖩 On your calculator, use the EXP or EE button for standard form.
- To add or subtract, convert numbers back to ordinary form.

To convert to standard form:
- Put the decimal point in position (ie to give a number between 1 and 10).
- Count how many moves to get the decimal point back to its original place.
- Moving to the right $\rightarrow$ positive power
- Moving to the left $\rightarrow$ negative power

If $x = 3.6 \times 10^4$ and $y = 1.8 \times 10^{-8}$, calculate the values of x^2 and x/y, giving your answers in the form $a \times 10^n$, where $1 \leq a \leq 10$ and $n \in \mathbb{Z}$.

(The last bit is a fancy way of saying "answers in standard form.")
To multiply, multiply the first parts and add the powers. $(3.6 \times 10^4) \times (3.6 \times 10^4) = \underline{\mathbf{1.296 \times 10^9}}$
To divide, divide the first parts and subtract the powers. $(3.6 \times 10^4) \div (1.8 \times 10^{-8}) = \underline{\mathbf{2 \times 10^{12}}}$

Let $s = 81000$ and $t = 0.012$. Write s and t in standard form, and calculate $s \div t$, giving your answer in standard form.

YOU SOLVE

$\underline{8.1 \times 10^4,\ 1.2 \times 10^{-2},\ 6.75 \times 10^6}$

Units of Measurement

The metric system: The basic units of measurement are:

Quantity	Unit	Symbol
Length	Metre	m
Weight	Gramme	g
Time	Second	s
Liquid volume	Litre	l

Using prefixes, all of these units can be increased or decreased in multiples of 10. The common prefixes are:

Smaller	Power of 10	Bigger
deci (d)	10^1	deca (D)
centi (c)	10^2	hecta (h)
milli (m)	10^3	kilo (k)
micro (μ)	10^6	mega (M)

eg: 1000 millilitres = 1 litre (1000ml = 1l)
       100 centimetres = 1 metre (100cm = 1m)
       1000 grammes = 1 kilogram (1000g = 1kg)

When the units are combined, use the following notation
eg: Speed = metres per second = ms^{-1}

You will often find standard form useful for converting units. For example, to convert kilometres to millimetres you will need to multiply by 1000 and 1000 again, ie by 10^6. So, 4km = 4×10^6mm.

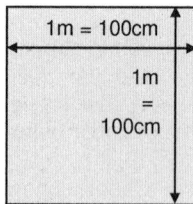

Areas and volumes: How many cm^2 is $4m^2$? It is tempting to multiply by 100 and say $400cm^2$. However, as we can see from the square, $1m^2 = 100cm^2 \times 100cm^2 = 10000cm^2$.
So, $4m^2 = 4 \times 100 \times 100 = 40000cm^2$. Use a similar calculation for volumes.

eg: $3.1cm^3 = 3.1 \times 10 \times 10 \times 10 = 3100mm^3$

```
1m = 100cm

1m
=
100cm
```

Note that for water, $1ml = 1cm^3$. It follows that $1litre = 1000cm^3$ and, since $1m^3 = 1,000,000cm^3$, $1m^3 = 1000$ litres.

Conversions: How do we convert a speed of, say, $65kmh^{-1}$ to ms^{-1}? 1km = 1000m and 1 hour = 3600s, so the calculation is going to involve multiplications and/or divisions of these numbers. Think like this:
- In 1 hour, the number of metres travelled will be a bigger number than the number of km – so *multiply* by 1000.
- In 1 second, the distance travelled will be less than in 1 hour, so *divide* by 3600.
- $65kmh^{-1} = \dfrac{65 \times 1000}{3600} = 18.1ms^{-1}$

Estimations: Answers can be estimated by using 1 S.F. throughout, and you should always check your answers are *reasonable* by doing such an estimate (see page 6).
eg: The radius of the Earth is about 6400km. How fast is a point on the equator travelling in ms^{-1}? The calculation required is:

speed = $\dfrac{2\pi \times 6400 \times 1000}{24 \times 3600} \approx \dfrac{6 \times 6000 \times 1000}{20 \times 4000} = \dfrac{36000}{80} \approx 400ms^{-1}$

Required data:
1 day = 24 hours
1 hour = 3600s
1km = 1000m

Required formulae:
$C = 2\pi r$
Speed = distance/time

The actual answer is $465.4ms^{-1}$

Sequences and Series

There are many different types of number sequence. You only need to know about two: the *arithmetic sequence* (AP) and the *geometric sequence* (GP). In an AP each number is the previous number *plus* a constant. In a GP each number is the previous number *multiplied* by a constant.

A *series* is the same as a *sequence* except that the terms are added together: thus a series has a *sum*, whereas a sequence doesn't.

To answer most sequences and series questions, make sure you are familiar with the formulae below. First, the notation:

a = the first term of the sequence
n = the number of terms in the sequence
l = the last term of the sequence
d = the common difference (the number added on in an AP)
r = the common ratio (the multiplier in a GP)
u_n = the value of the nth term
S_n = the sum of the first n terms

The formulae:
For an AP:

The value of the nth term: $u_n = a + (n-1)d$

The sum of n terms: $S_n = \dfrac{n}{2}(a + l) = \dfrac{n}{2}(2a + (n-1)d)$

For a GP:

The value of the nth term: $u_n = ar^{n-1}$

The sum of n terms: $S_n = \dfrac{a(r^n - 1)}{r - 1}$

> *Examples:*
>
> *Arithmetic sequences:*
> 3, 5, 7, 9 .....
> 1.1, 1.3, 1.5, 1.7 .....
> 11, 7, 3, -1, -5 ......
>
> *Geometric Sequences:*
> 1, 3, 9, 27 .....
> 4, 6, 9, 13.5 .....
> 12, 6, 3, 1.5, 0.75 .....

> Your formula sheet uses u_1 instead of a.

> The sum formulae always start from the first term. If you wanted to sum, say, the 10th to the 20th terms, you would calculate $S_{20} - S_9$. Think about it!

At the end of 1983 the population of a town was k people. At the end of 1999 the population was $5k$ people after an average increase of 70 people each year. Calculate k.
This is an A.P. because 70 people are *added* each year. Count the number of terms carefully, using your fingers if necessary! – 1999 will be the 17th term.

$u_{17} = k + (17 - 1) \times 70$ but $u_{17} = 5k$
$5k = k + 1120 \Rightarrow 4k = 1120 \Rightarrow \underline{\textbf{k = 280}}$

A ball is dropped from a height of 9m. It hits the ground and rebounds to a height of 6m. It falls again, hits the ground and rebounds to a height of 4m. It continues to fall, hit the ground and rebound with its rebound height and fall height in the same ratio.
a)   To what height will it rebound after it next hits the ground?
b)   How many times will it hit the ground before the rebound height becomes less than 9cm?
a) G.P. since the height is multiplied each time. To find the multiplier, divide the second number by the first.
b) Note the change in units. Keep doing the sum on your calculator and count the number of hits on the ground.

YOU SOLVE

<u>2.67m</u>,   <u>**12 hits**</u>

Simple and Compound Interest

One important application of sequences and series is their use in solving financial problems involving *interest*. If a sum of money is invested, the interest is the amount (expressed as a %) that it earns during each period (usually, but not necessarily, a year).

Simple interest: The interest earned is not added to the amount invested which thus stays constant.

- $1000 at 5% simple interest per year will earn $50/year. In 10 years, the investment is worth 1000 + 10 x 50 = $1500.

Compound interest: The interest earned is *added* to the amount invested. Thus the investment grows by a larger amount each year.

- $1000 at 5% compound interest will multiply by 1.05 each year (A 5% increase can be calculated using a multiplier of 1.05).

After 1 year, the investment is worth 1000 x 1.05 = $1050

After 2 years, the investment is worth 1050 x 1.05 = $1102.50

After n years, the investment is worth 1000×1.05^n

Beware of questions where extra money is added to the investment each year *as well as* the interest.

Note that with the simple interest, the value of the investment is increased by $50/year and will form an AP. With the compound interest, the value will x 1.05 each year and will form a GP.

John deposits $2500 with a bank which pays compound interest at a rate of 5% each year. Calculate the interest he receives at the end of four years.

His investment will be worth 2500×1.05^4 = $3038.77. So the amount of interest he has received will be 3038.77 − 2500 = **$538.77**

Amy invests $2500 with a company that pays simple interest annually. Calculate the rate of interest the company must pay in order that Amy receives the same interest as John after 4 years.

The amount of simple interest is the same each year, so it must be 538.77 ÷ 4 = $134.69. We now need this as a percentage of the investment.

$$\frac{134.69}{2500} \times 100 = \underline{\textbf{5.39\%}}$$

YOU SOLVE

Tino deposits $2000 into an investment account that pays 5% interest per annum.

a) **What will be the value of the investment after 6 years if the interest is reinvested**
(ie 5 years at 5% compound interest)

b) **How many years would it take the investment to double in value.**
(Keep multiplying by 1.05 on your calculator)

c) **At the beginning of the each year Brenda deposits $2000 into an investment account that pays 5% interest per annum. Interest is calculated annually and reinvested. How much would be in the account after 6 years.**
(Don't worry about formulae: multiply by 1.05, then add 2000. Do this until 5 years are up).

$2680.19, 15 years, $14284.02

A loan of $4000 at a rate of 12% per annum is compounded monthly. How much will it cost if the loan is to be repaid in 1 year?

Each month 1% interest is added to the loan, so the total for the year will be more than 12%.

Cost for 1 year = 4000×1.01^{12} = **4507.30**

What is the equivalent simple interest rate?

Total interest = $507.30, so the rate is $\dfrac{507.30}{4000} \times 100 = \underline{\textbf{12.7\%}}$

Simultaneous Equations

The process of solving equations enables us to find the values of unknown quantities. Commonly, equations are solved using algebra; other methods are sometimes used, including graphical techniques. If there are *two* unknown quantities, we require two equations to find them. Such equations are called *simultaneous* because we are finding the pair of values which will satisfy both equations at the same time, or simultaneously. There are two algebraic methods which are commonly used.

Elimination: Elimination is generally used when the pattern of the two equations is the same.

Solve: $2x - 3y = 11$ (1)
       $3x + 5y = 7$ (2)

$6x - 9y = 33$ (3) = (1) × 3   *(Choose multiplications which give*
$6x + 10y = 14$ (4) = (2) × 2   *the same number of x's or y's)*

$19y = \text{-}19$ (4) - (3)
$y = \text{-}1$

Now we must find x as well. Substitute the value of y into either of the original equations (2) looks easier.

$3x + 5 \times \text{-}1 = 7$
$3x = 12$
$x = 4$

<u>So the solution is $x = 4$, $y = \text{-}1$</u>

> Note that it is good practice to put the full answer at the end of the question rather than leaving part of it tucked away in the middle.

Substitution: This is a more general method, and is particularly easy to use if at least one of the equations is in the form $y =$ or $x =$.

Solve: $y = 3x - 5$ (1)
       $6x + 2y = \text{-}1$ (2)

Substitute (1) into (2)
$7x + 2(3x - 5) = \text{-}1$ *Now solve as an ordinary linear equation*
$6x + 6x - 10 = \text{-}1$
$12x = 9$
$x = 0.75$

Substitute the value of x into (1)
$y = 3 \times 0.75 - 5$
$y = \text{-}2.75$

<u>So the solution is $x = 0.75$, $y = \text{-}2.75$</u>

Graphical solution: Since each of the simultaneous equations (of the type in the examples above) represent straight lines, the point of intersection represents the only value of x and y which fits both equations. 🖩 Plot the graphs, and then use the calculator function which finds the point of intersection. The display below shows the calculator being used to solve $y = 2x - 2$ and $y = 4 - 0.5x$.

The solution is $x = 2.4$ and $y = 2.8$.

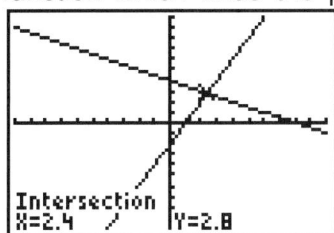

Intersection
X=2.4   Y=2.8

Quadratic Equations

What is a quadratic equation: A quadratic *expression* is in the form $ax^2 + bx + c$, where $a \neq 0$. The following are examples of quadratic expressions:

$$2x^2 - 3x + 5; \quad x^2 - 23; \quad -4x^2; \quad 6x^2 + 2x$$

So equations which involve such expressions are called *quadratic equations*. They are not as simple to solve as linear equations (eg: $2x - 3 = 6$) because it is harder to make x the subject. To further complicate things, there are usually two possible solutions for x. You are expected to be able to use factorisation or graphs to solve quadratic equations.

Factorisation: Factorising is the opposite of multiplying out. Quadratic factorisation can come in three forms:

- **$ax^2 + bx$** - use common factors
  eg: $2x^2 - 6x = 2x(x - 3)$
- **$a^2x^2 - b^2$** - the "difference of two squares"
  eg: $x^2 - 36 = x^2 - 6^2 = (x - 6)(x + 6)$
  $4x^2 - 49 = (2x)^2 - 7^2 = (2x - 7)(2x + 7)$
  and you may have to use common factors first:
  eg: $2x^2 - 50 = 2(x^2 - 25) = 2(x - 5)(x + 5)$
  You just have to be able to recognise the types of expression which factorise like this. Note particularly that expressions of the form $x^2 + a^2$ do *not* factorise.
- **$x^2 + bx + c$** - factorise into two brackets. You must first find two numbers which add to give b and multiply to give c (taking signs into account)
  eg: $x^2 + 8x + 15$. The two numbers are 3 and 5, so:
  $x^2 + 8x + 15 = (x + 3)(x + 5)$
  eg: $x^2 - 3x - 10$. The two numbers are -5 and +2, so:
  $x^2 - 3x - 10 = (x - 5)(x + 2)$
  eg: $x^2 - 10x + 24$. The two numbers are -6 and -4, so:
  $x^2 - 10x + 24 = (x - 6)(x - 4)$

To solve a quadratic equation using factorisation, you must make sure that the equation has 0 on the right hand side. If necessary, you must rearrange the equation first. In factorised form, equations solve like this:

- $(x - 6)(x - 4) = 0 \Rightarrow x = 4$ or 6
- $(x - 5)(x + 2) = 0 \Rightarrow x = 5$ or -2
- $2x(x - 3) = 0 \Rightarrow x = 0$ or 3
- $(x + 6)(x - 6) = 0 \Rightarrow x = -6$ or 6

> The simplest quadratic equation is of the form
> $$x^2 = 25$$
> in which case the solution is
> $$x = \pm 5.$$
> Don't forget that there are always 2 square roots.

> Difference of two squares
>
> The factorisation derives from the fact that
> $$(a - b)(a + b) = a^2 - b^2$$

> This is because if $p \times q = 0$ it follows that either $p = 0$ or $q = 0$. So in the first example, either $x - 6 = 0$ or $x - 4 = 0$, giving $x = 6$ or 4.

A rectangular garden is fenced on three sides using 80m of fencing. The fourth side is an existing brick wall. Take x metres to represent the length of one of the sides of the garden at right angles to the wall.

a) Draw a diagram of the garden, labelling the lengths of the sides in terms of x.

b) If the area of the garden is 600m^2, find its dimensions given that the brick wall represents the longer side.

a) The two short sides are each length x, so that leaves the remaining length of fencing as $80 - 2x$.

b) Area = length × width = 600, so $x(80 - 2x) = 600$
This gives $80x - 2x^2 = 600 \Rightarrow 2x^2 - 80x + 600 = 0$
(The rearrangement has put 0 on the RHS, and made the x^2 term +ve.)
Common factor first: $2(x^2 - 40x + 300) = 0$
$2(x - 30)(x - 10) = 0$, so $x = 30$ or 10
Substituting gives dimensions of 30m × 20m or 10m × 60m (Check: both give area = 600)
The brick wall is longer, so the dimensions of the garden are **10m × 60m**

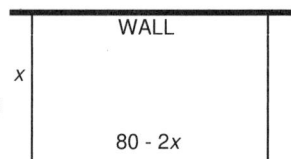

Quadratic graphs: The graph of $y = ax^2 + bx + c$ will always be a parabola, whatever the values of a, b and c. A parabola is a curve where both sides get ever closer to the vertical.

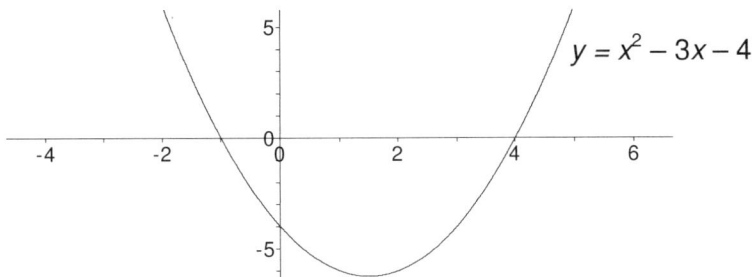

$y = x^2 - 3x - 4$

The points on the graph above can be worked out by drawing up a table. The y coordinates are calculated by adding up the three previous columns.

x	x^2	$-3x$	-4	y
-2	4	6	-4	6
-1	1	3	-4	0
0	0	0	-4	-4
1	1	-3	-4	-6
2	4	-6	-4	-6
3	9	-9	-4	-4
4	16	-12	-4	0
5	25	-15	-4	6

The solutions of the equation $x^2 - 3x - 4 = 0$ will be the values of x where the graph intersects the x-axis, and we can see that these fall at $x = -1$ and $x = 4$. This is particularly helpful when the quadratic does not factorise, leading to non-integer solutions.

The converse is also true: if we solve the equation by factorisation, the solutions will be the point where the graph cuts the x-axis.

▤ You can solve quadratic equations either by drawing the graph on the calculator and finding where it cuts the x-axis, or by writing a program which uses the quadratic formula. The formula is not in the syllabus, but you may use it to solve quadratic equations.

Terminology: The x values where a graph cuts the axis are known as *zeros* or *roots*.

YOU SOLVE

a)   **Solve the equation $x^2 - 5x + 6 = 0$.**

b)   **Find the coordinates of the points where the graph of $y = x^2 - 5x + 6$ intersects the x-axis.** *(The answer to this can be written down without drawing the graph)*

$\underline{x = 3 \text{ or } 2, \quad (3, 0) \text{ and } (2, 0)}$

a)   **Factorise the expression $x^2 - 2x - 8$.**
b)   **For what range of integer values of x is $x^2 - 2x - 8$ less than 0.**

a) $\underline{x^2 - 2x - 8 = (x - 4)(x + 2)}$
b)   Look at the graph:
       The y values represent the values of $x^2 - 2x - 8$. When are these values less than 0? When the graph is below the axis. And between what values of x does this happen?
       $\underline{-2 < x < 4}$

SETS, LOGIC AND PROBABILITY

Definitions and notation: Set theory encompasses a wide range of mathematical (and non-mathematical) fields, and it has its own language. A set is any collection of things with a common property: it can be *finite* (eg: set of students in a class) or infinite (eg: set of integers). A set is denoted by a capital letter, and can be defined in words or as a list.

- A = even numbers between 1 and 9
- A = {2, 4, 6, 8}

Note the use of "curly brackets" to list the members of a set.

or a special notation can be used:

- A = {x | x is an even number between 1 and 9}. This would be read as: "The set A is a list of things called x where x is an even number between 1 and 9."

You must be familiar with the following list of symbols:

Symbol	Meaning	Example
U	universal set	U = all the books on my bookshelf.
$\in$	is a member of	E = even numbers; $4 \in A$
$\notin$	is not a member of	E = even numbers; $5 \notin A$
'	complementary set	E = even numbers, E' = odd numbers
$\varnothing$	empty (null) set	A = odd numbers divisible by 2; A = $\varnothing$
$\cap$	intersection	B = multiples of 2; C = multiples of 3 B $\cap$ C = multiples of 6
$\cup$	union	T = tea drinkers; C = coffee drinkers T $\cup$ C = those who drink tea or coffee or both
$\subset$	is a subset of	F = multiples of 4; T = multiples of 2; F$\subset$T
$n(A)$	number of elements in set A	A = {1,3,6,8,9}; $n(A)$ = 5

Brackets can be used with the same meaning as in algebra. Thus, (A $\cap$ B)' = the complement of set A $\cap$ B, but:
A' $\cap$ B' = the complement of set A $\cap$ the complement of set B
The difference between these can be seen if we define
$$U = \{1,2,3,4,5,6\}, \quad A = \{2,5,6\}, \quad B = \{1,2,3,4\}$$

So, A' = {1,3,4}, B' = {5,6} and A $\cap$ B = {2}
Thus, (A $\cap$ B)' = {1,3,4,5,6} but A' $\cap$ B' = $\varnothing$

Sentences: Set notation can be translated into English sentences, but to have meaning they need a "verb". The equivalents to verbs are: =, $\neq$, $\in$, $\notin$, $\subset$, $\not\subset$

U = {members of 1997 IB class in school X}
F = {members who play football}
M = {members who passed the last math test}
L = {members who speak three languages}

a) Express as sentences: (i) L $\cup$ F = U (ii) L $\cap$ M = M

i) L $\cup$ F are all those who either speak 3 languages or play football or both. Since this group is equal to the whole class, it follows that: **"Everyone in the class either speaks 3 languages or plays football or both."** (It's a bit cumbersome as a sentence, but could be a lot worse)!

ii) L $\cap$ M are those who both passed the test and speak 3 languages. Since this is exactly the same group who passed the test, we know that: **"All those who passed the test speak 3 languages."** (It is also true that M $\subset$ L, and this equivalent to L $\cap$ M = M).

b) Express in set language: "There is no-one who speaks 3 languages and plays football."

Putting this partially into set language we can say: "The set of those who speak 3 languages and play football is empty." So, **L $\cap$ F = $\varnothing$**. Note that L $\neq$ F is not the same at all – it simply says that the set of those speaking 3 languages is different from the set of those who play football.

Venn Diagrams

In a room there are 20 people. 11 have black hair, 6 have glasses. 2 people have both black hair and glasses. Imagine that we draw two circles on the floor labelled "black hair" and "glasses" and ask the people to stand in the appropriate circle. The circles will have to overlap to allow for the two people with both. The numbers of people in each region of the room will be:

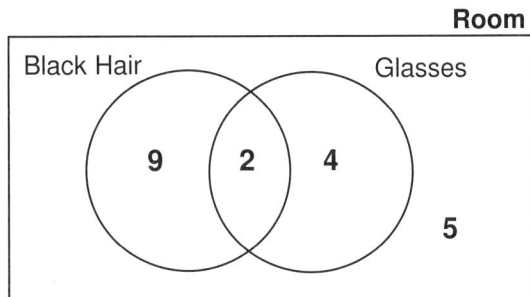

This is a Venn Diagram. The "room" represents the universal set – for a particular question, there is nothing outside. Each circle represents a set, the overlap is the intersection.

Room

Black Hair   Glasses

9   2   4

5

Points to note when filling in the numbers in a Venn Diagram:
- Start at the centre. If you are not told how many in the intersection, work it out like this: suppose you know there are 15 people in total in the two circles, 10 in circle A and 8 in circle B. 10 + 8 = 18, 3 more than 15 – there are 3 in the intersection.
- When we were told that there were 11 people with black hair, this *includes* those with both black hair and glasses. Same with the 6 people with glasses.

Don't forget to fill in the outer region – although in some questions this set will be "empty."

The diagrams on the right show how a Venn diagram can be shaded to show various sets. To find an intersection, you can shade the two sets in different directions, and the intersection will be the area with cross shading. To find a union, shade the two sets in the same direction – the union is the complete shaded area.

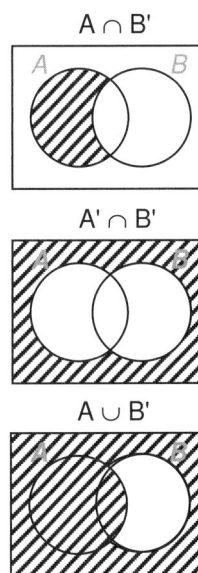

$A \cap B'$

$A' \cap B'$

$A \cup B'$

Special cases:

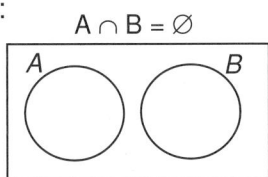

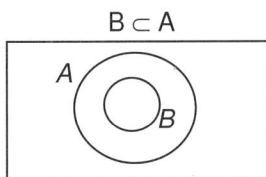

$A \cap B = \varnothing$

A   B

$B \subset A$

A

B

Alternatives to $B \subset A$ are:
$A \cap B = B$
$A \cup B = A$

Sometimes you are asked to fill in the regions of the Venn diagram with the actual elements in a set:

YOU SOLVE

U = {positive integers less than 10}
A= {integers that are multiples of 3}
B = {integers that are factors of 30}
List the elements of A and B and place them in the appropriate region in the Venn diagram. *(Some of this has been done for you).*

A = {......, ..., ...}   B = {......, ..., ..., ..., ...}

A   B

3

5

4

A group of 30 children are asked which of the three sports football (F), baseball (B) or volleyball (V) they play. The results are as follows:

2 children do not play any of these sports
3 children play all three sports
4 play volleyball and baseball
8 play football and baseball
7 play football and volleyball
16 play baseball
14 play volleyball

a) **Draw a Venn diagram to illustrate the relationship between the three sports played.**
b) **On your Venn diagram indicate the number of children that belong to each region.**
c) **How many children play only football?**

a) The Venn diagram consists of 3 intersecting circles, each labelled, and inside a rectangle.

b) Start by filling in the 2 who do not play sports – they go outside the circles. This leaves a total of 28 to be filled in inside the circles. Do we know the very centre, the intersection of all 3 sports? – yes, there are 3 children there. These 3 are *included* in the 4 who play volleyball and baseball, so we can fill in a 1 for the rest of the intersection of these two. Then do the same for the remaining intersections.

Now there are 16 who play baseball – including the 9 we already have. So 7 play *only* baseball. Similarly for volleyball. The total inside the circles is now 26, and we are expecting 28. The remaining region (only football) must therefore be 2.

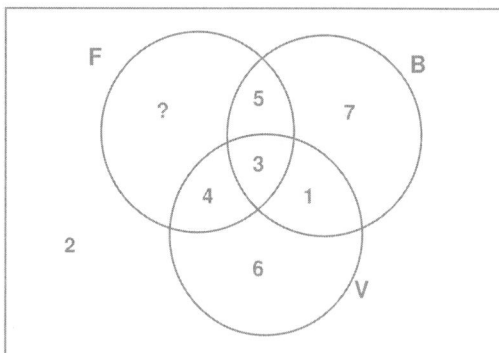

You should draw the Venn diagram for yourself and try filling it in.

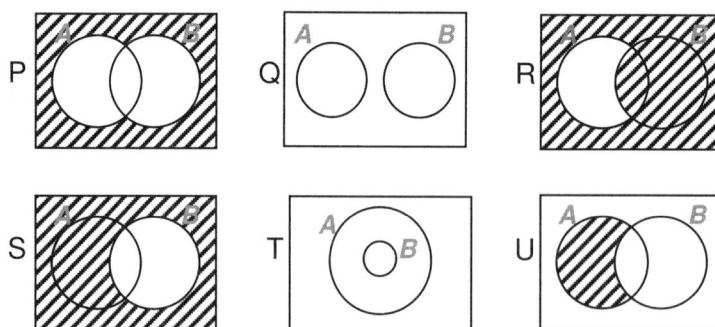

a) **Ignoring the shading, which of the diagrams illustrates**
   i) $A \cup B = A$; (ii) $A \cap B = \varnothing$
b) **In which Venn diagram does the shading represent**
   i) **the complement of B; (ii) the complement of $A \cup B$?**

T, Q, S, P

Basics of Symbolic Logic

Propositions: The building block of logic is the *proposition*. This is a statement that can have one of two values, *true* or *false*. "I paint pictures" and "$x > 4$" are propositions, whereas "What is the time?" and "$2x - 3$" are not. Propositions can be denoted by a small letter.

Logic does not really concern itself with whether the propositions are *actually* true or false – only the reasoning leading from one proposition to the next.

eg: p: $x > 4$ reads as "p is the proposition that $x > 4$"

Negation: The *negation* of a proposition is formed by putting in words such as "not" or "do not." Its symbol is ¬.

- p: "I paint pictures"   ¬p: "I do not paint pictures"
- p: "The train is late"   ¬p: "The train is not late"
- p: $x > 4$ ¬p: $x \leq 4$

Note that negation is not the same as "opposite." For example:

- p: "The glass is full"   ¬p: "The glass is not full"

You could not use "The glass is empty" because if the glass is not full, it could still have *some* water in it.

Truth tables: A truth table shows how the values (ie true or false) of a set of propositions affect the values of other propositions. The truth table for negation looks like this:

P	¬p
T	F
F	T

The first column shows all the possible values of p (ie true or false). The second column shows the corresponding values of ¬p. So take, for example, p: "The sun is shining". If p is true, and the sun is shining, then the proposition ¬p (ie "the sun is not shining") must be false, and vice versa.

Conjunction: The word *and* can be used to join two propositions together. Its symbol is ∧. For example:

- p: x is a positive even number. q: $x < 10$
- $p \wedge q$: x is a positive number and $x < 10$.

Clearly this combined proposition is only true when *both* of the original propositions are true. In other words, its truth table is:

P	q	p ∧ q
T	T	T
T	F	F
F	T	F
F	F	F

Note that we now need 4 rows to show all the possible combinations of values of p and q

Disjunction (alternation):

The word *or* can also be used to join propositions. "Or" can mean two things: "One or the other or both" (disjunction with symbol ∨) or "one or the other but *not* both" (exclusive disjunction with symbol ⊻) Look carefully at their truth tables.

P	q	p ∨ q	p ⊻ q
T	T	T	F
T	F	T	T
F	T	T	T
F	F	F	F

Which of these two statements is disjunction, and which is exclusive disjunction?

- Your birthday party will either be this Saturday or next Saturday.
- This course requires you to have either a 5 in English or a 6 in History.

What is the truth table for the statement ¬p ∨ q ? We start by drawing up the first two columns as in the truth tables above, then drawing a third column for ¬p. Now we look at columns ¬p and q: when they are both false, ¬p ∨ q is false, otherwise it is true.

P	q	¬p	¬p ∨ q
T	T	F	T
T	F	F	F
F	T	T	T
F	F	T	T

Only FF will give F when drawing up a truth table for ∨

Implication

If...then...: Under what conditions is the proposition *r:* "If you steal then you will go to prison" true? Clearly if you *do* steal and you *do* go to prison, then *r* is true. However, if you steal and you *don't* go to prison (perhaps the judge was feeling lenient) then *r* is false. If you *don't* steal that does not change the truth of *r*. Proposition *r* is an example of *implication*. The two propositions:

- *p*: "You steal"
- *q*: "You go to prison"

are joined by the words "if....then..." and the symbol is $\Rightarrow$. In other words, $r = p \Rightarrow q$ with truth table as shown on the right. The way to remember this truth table is that the row with TF → F, otherwise we get T.

p	*q*	$p \Rightarrow q$
T	T	T
T	F	F
F	T	T
F	F	T

Other possible wordings for $p \Rightarrow q$ are:

- *p* only if *q*
- *p* is sufficient for *q*
- *q* is necessary for *p*

eg: *p*: "*x* is a multiple of 4"   *q*: "*x* is a even"

$p \Rightarrow q$: "If *x* is a multiple of 4 then *x* is even" or
        "*x* is a multiple of 4 only if *x* is even" or
        "*x* is a multiple of 4 is sufficient for *x* to be even" or
        "*x* is even is necessary for *x* to be a multiple of 4"

Converse, inverse and contrapositive: Consider the following propositions:

- *p*: *x* = 16
- *q*: *x* is a square number

If *x* = 16 then *x* is a square number, so $p \Rightarrow q$ is true. But if *x* is square, does it follow that it is 16? This is the *converse* $q \Rightarrow p$ and is clearly not true. The *inverse* is $\neg p \Rightarrow \neg q$, ie If $x \neq 16$ then *x* is not a square number. Again, this is not true. But the *contrapositive*, which is $\neg q \Rightarrow \neg p$ (If *x* is not a square number then $x \neq 16$) *is* true. Let's put all these in one big truth table, remembering that the $\Rightarrow$ sign only gives false in a true/false row (the arrow shows one example of this):

p	*q*	$\neg p$	$\neg q$	$p \Rightarrow q$	$q \Rightarrow p$	$\neg p \Rightarrow \neg q$	$\neg q \Rightarrow \neg p$
T	T	F	F	T	T	T	T
T	F	F	T	F	T	T	F
F	T	T	F	T	F	F	T
F	F	T	T	T	T	T	T

Implication and contrapositive have the same truth tables, so they are equivalent statements (that's why the contrapositive is true when the implication is true). It can also be seen that the converse and the inverse are equivalent. eg:

☐*p*: "I am wet"

☐*q*: "It is raining"

$p \Rightarrow q$ is not true (I could be wet because I have had a swim). However, if the statement $q \Rightarrow p$ ("If it is raining then I am wet") is true, then so is the inverse $\neg p \Rightarrow \neg q$ ("If I am not wet then it is not raining").

a) Complete the truth table given below:

p	q	¬p	p ⇒ q	q ⇒ ¬p
T	T	F	T	F
T	F	F	F	T
F	T	T	T	T
F	F	T	T	T

b) If *p* is true, what can you say about $(p \Rightarrow q) \wedge (q \Rightarrow \neg p)$?

This looks hard, but it breaks down quite easily. The two propositions in brackets are the ones for which we have just completed the truth tables. Now, what is the truth table for ∧? Always false except in the row with TT, ie TT → T. This happens in both of the last two rows. But we are told that *p* is true, and this happens only in the *first* two rows – these rows finish with TF and FT, so the ∧ is always false. So: $(p \Rightarrow q) \wedge (q \Rightarrow \neg p)$ **is false if *p* is true**.

(Note that we are dealing with pure logic – we do not need to know what *p* and *q* actually are).

YOU SOLVE

a) Complete the truth table for:

r: $x > 4$

s: $x^2 > 16$

r	s	¬r	¬r ∨ s
T	T		
T	F		
F	T		
F	F		

b) Using the results of part (a), is $\neg r \vee s$ true, or false, when:

i) $x > 4$ and $x^2 \not> 16$

ii) $x \not> 4$ and $x^2 > 16$ *The symbol ≯ means "not greater than."*

i) <u>False</u>   ii) <u>True</u>

---

p: *x* is a multiple of 6; *q*: *x* is a multiple of 5; *r*: *x* is a factor of 60

a)   i) Write a sentence, in words, for the statement: $(q \vee r) \wedge \neg p$

The problem is the bracket: generally, in statements, "and" takes precedence over "or", but we need to bracket the *q* and the *r*. Here's one possibility, with the "or" understood to be inclusive: <u>"*x* is a multiple of 5 or a factor of 60, and *x* is not a multiple of 6."</u>

ii) Write in logic notation: "If *x* is a factor of 60 then it is either not a multiple of 6 or it is a multiple of 5."

We can see an if...then.. in the sentence, so we go for implication: <u>$r \Rightarrow \neg p \vee q$</u>

b)   i) Complete the truth table to determine the truth values of each of the following two statements: $(q \vee r) \wedge \neg p$; $r \Rightarrow p \vee \neg q$

The columns are methodically built up to produce the complex statements. Remember the basics: For ∧, TT → T, otherwise F; for ∨, FF → F, otherwise T; for ⇒, TF → F otherwise T.

p	q	r	¬p	q ∨ r	(q ∨ r) ∧ ¬p	¬q	p ∨ ¬q	r ⇒ p ∨ ¬q
T	T	T	F	T	F	F	T	T
T	T	F	F	T	F	F	T	T
T	F	T	F	T	F	T	T	T
T	F	F	F	F	F	T	T	T
F	T	T	T	T	T	F	F	F
F	T	F	T	T	T	F	F	T
F	F	T	T	T	T	T	T	T
F	F	F	T	F	F	T	T	T

ii)   a) List the combinations of truth values of *p*, *q* and *r* that make the statement $(q \vee r) \wedge \neg p$ true. <u>FTT, FTF and FFT</u>

b) Write down a possible value of *x* for each of these combinations of truth values.

We now need to compare the truth values with the original statements. Possible values of *x* are:
For FTT, <u>*x* = 10</u>. For FTF, <u>*x* = 25</u>. For FFT, <u>*x* = 3</u>

Equivalence, Tautology and Contradiction

Equivalence: If two statements have the same truth tables then they are true and false under exactly the same conditions. In this case they are *equivalent* statements. The symbol is $\Leftrightarrow$ and the wording is one of:

- if and only if
- is necessary and sufficient

eg: p: "x is a multiple of 2" ; q: "x is even"

Clearly both $p \Rightarrow q$ and $q \Rightarrow p$ are both true, so $p \Leftrightarrow q$ and we can write "x is a multiple of 2 if and only if x is even." The *if* works forwards, and the *only if* works backwards.

P	q	$p \Leftrightarrow q$
T	T	T
T	F	F
F	T	F
F	F	T

A question might ask under what conditions two complex statements are equivalent. We build up their truth tables, and where they have *different* truth values, we say that those rows are not allowed. (eg: The answer might be "equivalent except when p is true, q is false and r is true").

YOU SOLVE

p: The car is old q: The car is not green r: The car is a station wagon.

a)   **Express in logic notation**
   i)   The car is not old.
   (ii)   The car is green if and only if it is not old and a station wagon
b)   **Write the following statement as a sentence in words** $(\neg r \wedge q) \Rightarrow \neg p$

a) $\neg p$, $\neg q \Leftrightarrow \neg p \wedge r$ b) If the car is not a station wagon and is green then it is new
(Be safe: don't try and make the English better. eg: "Not a station wagon and not green" is not the same as saying "not a green station wagon.")

Tautology and contradiction: A tautology is a statement that *always* has the value true, whatever the values of the original propositions. ie its truth table is all T's. And a contradiction is *always* false, its truth table being all F's. For example, the truth table for : $(p \Rightarrow q) \Leftrightarrow (p \wedge \neg q)$ is:

P	q	$p \Rightarrow q$	$\neg q$	$p \wedge \neg q$	$(p \Rightarrow q) \Leftrightarrow (p \wedge \neg q)$
T	T	T	F	F	F
T	F	F	T	T	F
F	T	T	F	F	F
F	F	T	T	F	F

So the statement is a contradiction – it is never true.

Analogy between sets and logic: The set notation (eg: A', $\cap$, $\cup$) and logic notation ($\neg a$, $\wedge$, $\vee$) are very close to each other, and Venn diagrams can be used to illustrate logic. For example, if we draw a Venn diagram where set A represents multiples of 3, then the circle can also represent the proposition a: "x is a multiple of 3" with true values inside the circle, false values outside.

Probability Notation and Formulae

Notation: The *sample space* in a given situation is the set of all the things that can happen and is defined by the letter U. An *event* is one of the things that can happen and is given any other capital letter. A capital P stands for "probability", so we can shorten "the probability of event A" to P(A). The number of ways A can happen is denoted by $n(A)$. Probabilities are always numbers between 0 (definitely won't happen) and 1 (definitely will happen).

- $P(A) = \dfrac{n(A)}{n(U)}$

In other words, to find the probability of an event, divide the number of ways it can (or did) happen by the total number of possibilities.

The probability that event *A* does *not* happen is denoted by *A'*. It follows that

- $P(A) + P(A') = 1$

The set notation symbols $\cap$ and $\cup$ are used for the words "and" and "or" in probability.

A basket of fruit contains 10 apples, 6 bananas and 4 oranges. A fruit is selected at random.

a)   Find the probability that a fruit selected is not an orange.

There are 20 fruits of which 16 are not oranges so <u>P(not an orange) = 16/20 = 0.8</u>

b)   The first and second fruits selected are both bananas and they are eaten. Find the probability that the next fruit selected will be an apple.

There are now 18 fruits left of which 10 are still apples. <u>So P(apple) = 10/18</u>

Combined events: The probability of event *A or* event *B* happening (and this includes both) is calculated using addition.

- $P(A \cup B) = P(A) + P(B)$

but this formula works **only** if A and B are *mutually exclusive* – ie they cannot both happen at the same time. If they are not mutually exclusive, use:

- $P(A \cup B) = P(A) + P(B) - P(A \cap B)$

The probability of events A and B *both* happening is calculated by multiplication (remember that multiplying fractions gives a *smaller* answer and it is *less* likely that both events will happen than just one).

- $P(A \cap B) = P(A) \times P(B)$

but this formula works **only** if A and B are *independent* – ie one of them happening does not effect the probability of the other happening. If the events are not independent we are into the realms of *conditional probability* – ie the probability of one event happening if another has already happened. This is written as P(A|B), and read as "the probability of A given B."

- $P(A|B) = \dfrac{P(A \cap B)}{P(B)}$

A bag contains balls of two different colours. One is taken out, then another. The colour of the second is independent of the first if the first has been put back. If the first has been kept out, the colour of the second *depends* on the colour of the first.

Carlos travels each day by bicycle (probability 0.25), train (probability 0.65) or car. Find the probability that he travels

a)   by car on any day

b)   by bicycle on Thursday and Friday *("and" is multiply)*

c)   by bicycle on Monday and by train on Thursday

d)   either by train or by car on Monday and Tuesday. *(Consider "train or car" as a single event – what is its probability?)*

e)   by the same method of travel on Wednesday and Thursday. *(ie car and car or train and train or bicycle and bicycle).*   <u>0.1</u>,   <u>0.0625</u>,   <u>0.1625</u>,   <u>0.5625</u>,   <u>0.495</u>

YOU SOLVE

The formulae can be quite difficult to use, so only use them if you *have* to. Many probability questions can be solved by using appropriate diagrams as shown on the next few pages.

Lists and Tables of Outcomes

Lists: A list of possible outcomes is useful if there aren't too many of them. And it is important to ensure that each outcome in the list is equally likely. For example, when three coins are thrown, the possible combinations of heads and tails are:

HHH, HHT, HTH, HTT, THH, THT, TTH, TTT

If we want to find P(exactly two heads) we can see that there are three ways of achieving this (HHT, HTH, THH) so the probability is 3/8.

Five cards (numbered 1 to 5) are shuffled and two selected at random, one after the other.
a)   What is the probability that the number on the first card selected is larger than the number on the second card?
b)   What is the probability that the sum of the two numbers is divisible by 3?

There are few enough combinations to make it worthwhile listing *all* the possibilities.

12, 13, 14, 15, 21, 23, 24, 25, 31, 32, 34, 35, 41, 42, 43, 45, 51, 52, 53, 54

(The first card is *not* replaced, so 22 for example is not a possibility. And order matters, so 21 is different from 12).

a)   There are 20 combinations. 10 of them have the first number larger than the second. So probability = **10/20** (which can be deduced from common sense)!

b)   The following combinations are divisible by 3: 12, 15, 21, 24, 42, 45, 51, 54, so probability = **8/20**

Tables of outcomes: Tables of outcomes show how many ways two events can, or cannot, happen.

In a survey of 48 students it was found that 30 study Spanish and 13 study Maths. Six of those who study Spanish also study Maths.
a)   Copy and complete the table.

The 30 and the 13 will be totals, the 6 goes in the "study Spanish, study Maths box" – then the rest can be completed.

	Study Spanish	Do not study Spanish	Total
Study Maths	6	7	13
Do not study Maths	24	11	35
Total	30	18	48

b)   What is the probability that a student selected at random:
i)   studies Maths and studies Spanish?
ii)   studies Maths but does not study Spanish?
iii)   studies Maths if he studies Spanish?

i)   This applies to 6 students, so probability = **6/48**
ii)   This applies to 7 students, so probability = **7/48**

iii)   This is a conditional probability, but we do not need to use the formula. We *know* that the student studies Spanish and so is one of 30. Of these 30, 6 study Maths. Therefore, the probability = **6/30**

Venn Diagrams and Tree Diagrams

Venn Diagrams: These were introduced on page 15. They can be an extremely useful tool when solving probability questions. Take the example on page 15 where 20 people are in a room, some with black hair and some with glasses.

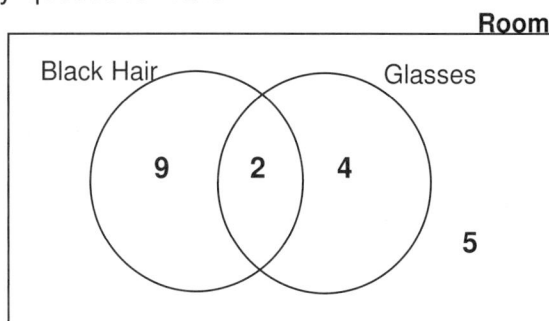

Once the data has been entered into the diagram, all probabilities associated with it can be easily calculated.

When someone is selected at random, the probability they have:

> Black hair and glasses = 2/20
> Black hair and no glasses = 9/20
> Not got glasses = 14/20
> Glasses or black hair (or both) = 15/20
> Glasses given black hair = 2/11 *(We know it's one of the 11 with black hair – and only 2 of these have got glasses)*
> Glasses given not black hair = 4/9

The Venn diagram shows the number of students in a year group at a school who have joined creative clubs. **A** is those who do Art, **M** is those who do Music, **P** is those who do Photography.

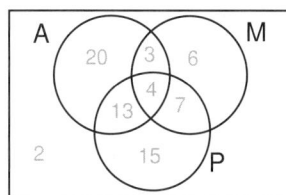

a) How many are there in the year group?
b) If a student is chosen at random, what is the probability that they:
  i) do Music;
  ii) do Art and Photography;
  ii) have not joined a creative club?
c) What is the probability that an artist is also a musician?

a) Adding up all the numbers gives **70**.
b) i) 20 do music altogether, so P(music) = **20/70**
    ii) There are 17 in the intersection of A and P, so P(art and photography) = **17/70**
    iii) There are 2 in the outer region, so P(have not joined any club) = **2/70**
c) This is conditional probability: we *know* that the person chosen is an artist. There are 40 in the art club altogether, and 7 of these are musicians. So P(M|A) = **7/40**

Tree diagrams: Tree diagrams are used to work out the probabilities for a *succession* of events. To find the probability of a set of successive branches, multiply each individual probability. To find the probability of one of several branches occurring, add the probabilities of each outcome.

Note that the probabilities associated with, say, taking two balls out of a bag simultaneously are the same as if the balls were taken out consecutively.

eg: P*(rains today)* = 0.3. If it rains today, P*(rains tomorrow)* = 0.65. However, if it is dry today, P*(rains tomorrow)* = 0.2 The tree diagram on the right shows the full set of possible outcomes and their associated probabilities.

Note the following points:
- Probabilities of branches coming out of one point add to give 1 since they cover all possibilities.
- The overall probabilities also add to give 1.

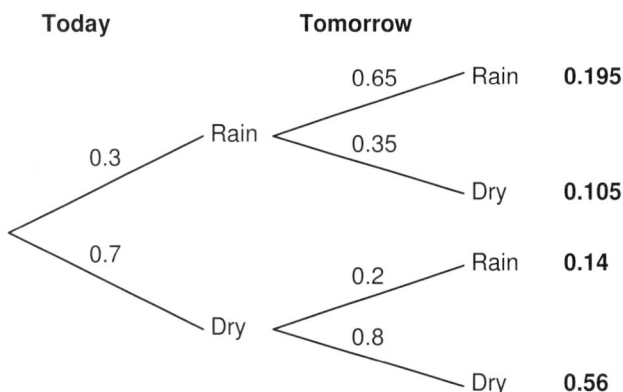

- The weather tomorrow is *not* independent of the weather today, hence the different probabilities depending on today's weather.

Some example probabilities are:
- P(two rainy days) = 0.195
- P(at least one rainy day) = 0.195 + 0.105 + 0.14 = 0.44
- P(exactly one rainy day) = 0.105 + 0.14 = 0.245

YOU SOLVE

In the senior class there are 20 boys and 26 girls.
a)   One student is selected randomly. What is the probability that a girl is selected?
How many students altogether? How many of them are girls?

b)   Two students are selected randomly to meet the school inspector. What is the probability that they are both of the same sex?
Draw a tree diagram which shows the four possible combinations. When putting the probabilities on the second set of branches, remember that one student has already been selected.

(a) <u>26/46</u>   (b) <u>103/207</u> or <u>0.498</u>

With and without replacement: In the question above, the probability of choosing two boys in part (b) is $\frac{20}{46} \times \frac{19}{45}$. This is because if a boy has been chosen first, there are then 19 boys left out of 45 students. Similarly, the P(two girls) = $\frac{26}{46} \times \frac{25}{45}$. The principle here is called "without replacement" since the first person chosen is not replaced in the group, and cannot be chosen again. In some questions you must read the question carefully to decide whether to use "with replacement" or "without replacement."

YOU SOLVE

a) A bag contains 6 green apples and 10 red apples. Without looking into the bag, Mary randomly selects one apple. What is the probability that it is green?

<u>6/16</u>

b) The apple is green and Mary eats it. The bag is passed to Oliver who randomly selects an apple – what is the probability that it is red?

<u>10/15</u>

c) The apple is red and Oliver replaces it in the bag. Now the bag is passed to Peter who randomly selects two apples. What is the probability they are both green?

<u>2/21</u>

FUNCTIONS

Basics of Functions

A function is an algebraic rule which shows how one set of numbers is related to, or obtained from another set. Functions often model real-life situations, so you must understand the different types of function and the notation and terminology used.

Defining functions: A function is defined using the notation f: $x \rightarrow$ ... eg f: $x \rightarrow x^2 - 1$. An alternative notation is $f(x) = x^2 - 1$ so that, for example, $f(3) = 3^2 - 1 = 8$. The x value put in to the function is called the *object* and the value of the function which results is called the *image*. Letters other than f and x can be used.

Read the definition as: "The function f takes any number x and turns it into $x^2 - 1$

Domain: The set of values to be put into a function is called the *domain* of the function. In many functions, *any* value can be input, in which case the domain is $x \in \mathbb{R}$. However, the domain may be restricted in a particular question. For example, suppose the x numbers in a function are limited to 3, 4 and 5, we can show the domain like this:

$$f: x \rightarrow 2x - 3, \ 3 \leq x \leq 5, \ x \in \mathbb{Z}$$

Range: The set of values produced by a function is called the *range*. For example, the function defined by f:$x \rightarrow x^2$ has a range $f(x) \geq 0$ since it is impossible for squares to be negative. Generally, the easiest way to find the range of a function is to look at its graph: the range is the complete set of possible y values.

Imagine a "function machine." When the handle is turned, the 5 drops in the top, and the function machine turns it into an 11!

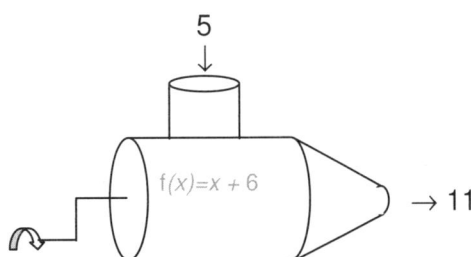

5
↓

$f(x) = x + 6$

→ 11

Mapping Diagram: A mapping diagram is a simple way to illustrate how members of the domain are "mapped" onto members of the range. For example, the mapping diagram below shows what happens to the numbers 0, 1 and 2 under the function $f(x) = 2x - 5$.

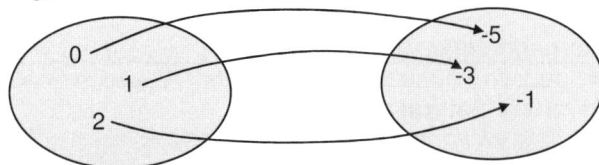

Functions do not have to be algebraic. For example, the diagram below could represent the function mapping sons onto fathers.

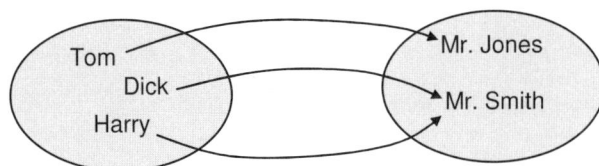

For a relationship to be a function, each member of the domain can only map on to *one* member of the range; but it is OK for different members of the domain to map onto the *same* member of the range. (So fathers → sons would not be a function since Mr.Smith has 2 sons).

Linear Functions

Burgers	Cost
1	1.50
2	3.00
3	4.50
4	6.00
5	7.50

Burgers cost £1.50 each. The table on the left shows how, as the number of burgers (x) increases steadily, so does the cost (y); the function connecting the two is *linear* because when the values are plotted on a graph the points form a straight *line*.

Equation of a straight line: *(see also page 33)* The equation of a straight line is usually written in one of two forms:

- $y = mx + c$ where m is the gradient of the line and c is the y-intercept (ie the point where the line cuts the y axis).
- $ax + by = c$ which is a rearrangement of the first form.

A line goes through (2, 3) and (5, 9) – what is its equation?

Gradient = $\dfrac{9 - 3}{5 - 2}$

So $y = 2x + c$
Substitute (2, 3)
$3 = 2 \times 2 + c \Rightarrow c = -1$
So equation is **$y = 2x - 1$**

OR

$y - 3 = 2(x - 2)$
$y - 3 = 2x - 4$
$y = 2x - 1$

Finding the equation of a line: To work out the equation of a line you need to know its gradient and a point. You can then either substitute into $y = mx + c$ or use the formula $y - y_1 = m(x - x_1)$ where (x_1, y_1) is the point. See examples on the left.

Drawing a line given its equation:

- Lines of the form $x = k$ are vertical
- Lines of the form $y = k$ are horizontal
- Lines of the form $y = kx$ go through (0, 0) and have gradient k (remember that a gradient of 2, for example, means that when the line goes along 1 it goes up 2)
- Lines of the form $y = mx + c$: put in two or three x values (eg: 0, 2 and 4) and work out the y values, then plot these as points. Join them up, continuing the line to both ends of the graph.
- Lines of the form $ax + by = c$: put $x = 0$ and work out y, then put $y = 0$ and work out x. Plot these two points and join them.

Important lines to remember:

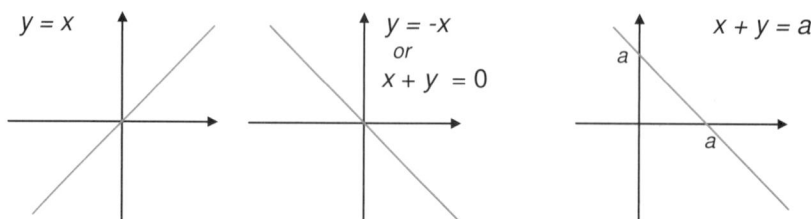

Intersection of lines: The point where two lines intersect can be worked out algebraically by solving a pair of simultaneous equations (see page 11).

The equation of line L is $y + 2x = 4$.
a) Find the gradient (slope) of L.
b) Find the gradient of a line perpendicular to L.
c) Find the equation of the line perpendicular to L which cuts the x-axis at −5.
d) Find where L and the line in part (c) intersect.

a) You must rearrange the equation to the form $y = mx + c$. So, $y = -2x + 4$, and we can see that the gradient of the line is **-2**.
b) Perpendicular lines have gradients which multiply to give −1. So the gradient will be **0.5**.
c) Note it cuts the x-axis at −5, not the y-axis. So we know the point (-5, 0) and the gradient 0.5. Substitute in the formula: $y - 0 = 0.5(x - (-5)) \Rightarrow$ **$y = 0.5x + 2.5$** or **$2y = x + 5$**
d) The point of intersection can be found by solving $y = -2x + 4$ and $y = 0.5x + 2.5$.
Subtracting gives $0 = -2.5x + 1.5 \Rightarrow x = 0.6$
Substituting into the first equation gives $y = -1.2 + 4 = 2.8$
So the point of intersection is **(0.6, 2.8)**

Quadratic Functions

The graph of a quadratic function has been mentioned on page 13 with regard to the solution of quadratic equations. The following notes relate to the general quadratic function $y = ax^2 + bx + c$

Properties of quadratic graphs: All quadratic graphs are parabolas, the sign of a determining "which way up." The value of c is the y-intercept. For example, the graph of $y = x^2 + 3x - 4$ cuts the y-axis at (0, -4) and is in the shape of a U. We can find the x-intercepts by factorising the equation:

- $y = x^2 + 3x - 4 \Rightarrow y = (x + 4)(x - 1)$ so the x-intercepts are at (0, -4) and (0 ,1)

The graph is always symmetrical about the vertical line passing through the vertex (turning point), a fact which can often be used when answering questions about the graph. The line of symmetry is always $x = \dfrac{-b}{2a}$

- $y = x^2 + 3x - 4$ has a line of symmetry at $x = -3/2 = -1.5$

The vertex is also on the line of symmetry, so its y-coordinate can be calculated by substituting into the equation:

- When $x = -1.5$, $y = (-1.5)^2 + 3 \times (-1.5) - 4 = -6.25$, so the vertex is at (-1.5, -6.25)

Summarising:

X INTERCEPTS
Solve the equation
$f(x) = 0$ by factorising

Y INTERCEPT
is the value of c

VERTEX
$x = -b/2a$
Find y by substituting x
into the equation

LINE OF SYMMETRY
$x = -b/2a$

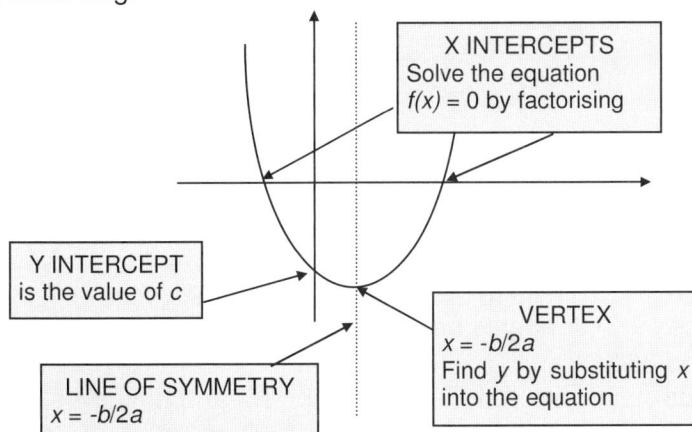

The symmetry of the graph comes in useful in all sorts of ways. For example, if you know that the graph crosses the x-axis at (0, 0) and at (4, 0), then the line of symmetry must be halfway between at $x = 2$.

Identify the diagram which best represents the graph of the each of the functions f(x) and g(x) where: a) f(x) = x² + 3x;   (b) g(x) = 3x − x²

Hint: Factorise the functions first – factorised form is much more useful. Where are the intercepts? Which way up is each graph?

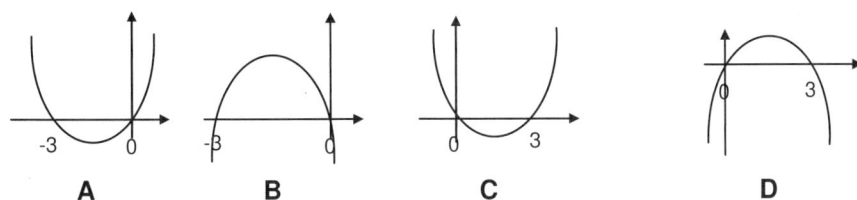

A   B   C   D

A   D

Sine and Cosine Functions

When using trigonometry to solve right angled triangles, we do not require the sine or cosine of any angle above 90°. However, this represents one small application of the sine and cosine functions which are in fact defined for *every* angle.

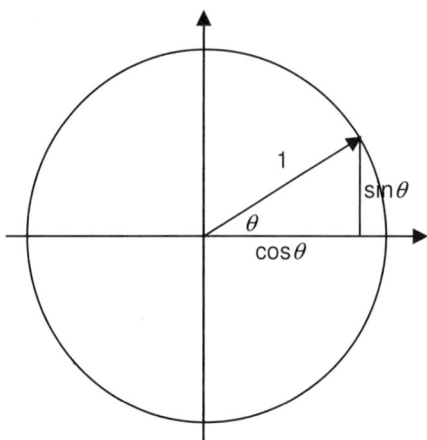

Sin and cos functions for all angles:
The diagram shows a circle with radius 1 (a *unit circle*). A line is drawn from the centre to a point on the circumference, and this forms angle θ with the x-axis. Then the x-coordinate of the point is defined as the cosine of the angle ($\cos\theta$) and the y-coordinate as the sine ($\sin\theta$). These definitions will apply as the line rotates full circle, giving the sin and cos for all angles from 0° to 360°. When these are plotted as graphs, we get the following:

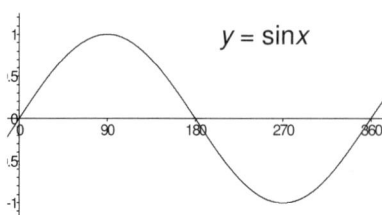

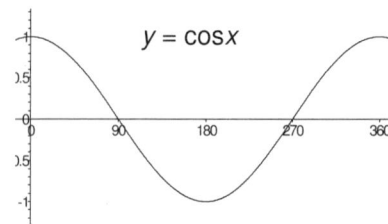

$y = \sin x$

$y = \cos x$

Points to note:
- The range of both functions is $-1 \le f(x) \le 1$
- $\sin x > 0$ for angles between 0° and 180°
- $\cos x > 0$ for angles between 0° and 90°, also between 270° and 360°
- Both functions have a *period* (ie repeat themselves) every 360°.

Graphs of other sine and cosine functions: How does the graph of $y = 2\sin x + 1$ compare to the graph of $y = \sin x$? Multiplying the sin function by 2 has the effect of *stretching* the graph by 2 in the y direction – that is, its range becomes –2 to 2. Adding 1 moves the whole curve up 1. The net effect is to end up with a curve with the same shape, but which:
- oscillates around $y = 1$
- has a maximum value of 3 and a minimum value of -1

> The size of the wave is called its *amplitude*. $y = \sin x$ has an amplitude of 1. $y = 2\sin x$ has an amplitude of 2

> The same rules can also be applied to the graph of $y = \cos x$

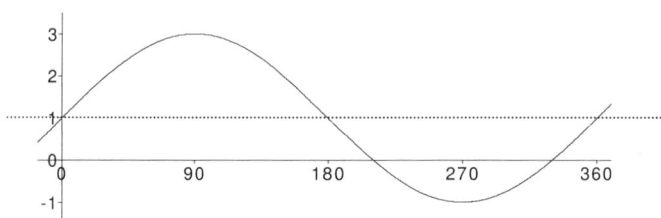

What happens if the *x* part of the function is multiplied by a number? For example, what does the graph of $y = \sin 2x$ look like?

This has the effect of doubling the *frequency* of the curve, making the wave go twice as fast. That is, its *period* (the *x* distance of one complete cycle) halves.

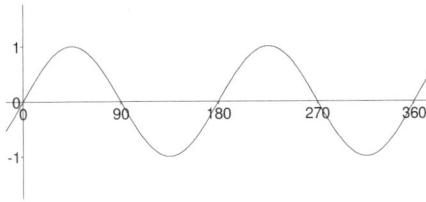

So the graph of $y = \sin(x/2)$ would have a period of 720°

In general, then, the graph of $y = a\sin bx + c$ will:
- Oscillate around $y = c$
- Have an amplitude of *a*
- Have a period of 360/*b*

Note that a value of −*a* will turn the graph upside down (ie reflect it in the *x*-axis).

The diagram below shows the graph of $y = p\sin x + q$. Use the graph to find the values of *p* and *q*.

First look for the centre of oscillation – this is the line $y = 1$. Now look to see how far above and below this line the graph goes: up to 4 and down to −2. So the amplitude is 3. Note too that the graph is "upside down".

Thus, **$p = -3$ and $q = 1$**

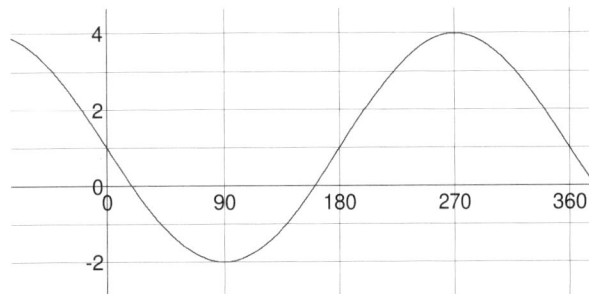

Applications: Many naturally occurring phenomena can be modelled using sine and cosine functions. Examples are: the length of the day through the year, the heights of tides through the day, the height of a bicycle pedal above the ground as it turns. If we are given the graph, we can solve problems relating to the real-life situation.

The temperature during a 24 hour period is illustrated on the graph and is given by the function $f : x \rightarrow a + 2\sin bt$, where *t* is the time in hours.

a) From the graph estimate the temperature after 9 hours.
b) What is the value of *a*?
c) What is the value of *b*?

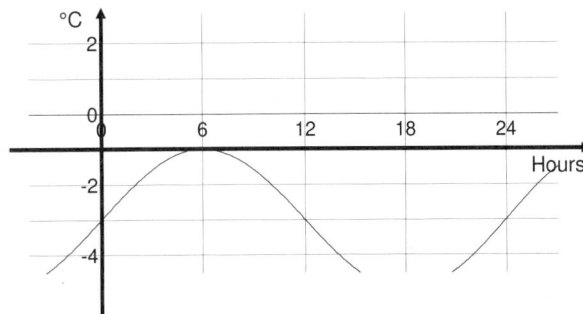

Don't be put off by the change of letter from y to t – the function still behaves in exactly the same way.

For part (c), look to see how long the period is – the time for one complete cycle. Then work out how many times faster that is compared to the 360° of y = sinx. This will be the value of b.

YOU SOLVE

<u>-1.6°,</u>   <u>a = -3,</u>   <u>b = 15</u>

Exponential Functions

Exponential functions are based on the function $f(x) = a^x$. Typical real life situations which can be modelled by exponential functions are population growth (eg: population increases by 1% per year) compound interest (eg: investment increases by 6% per year) and radioactive decay (eg: mass decreases by 10% every 30 years). One important feature of any exponential function is that the time taken to multiply by a certain amount (say, double) is always the same.

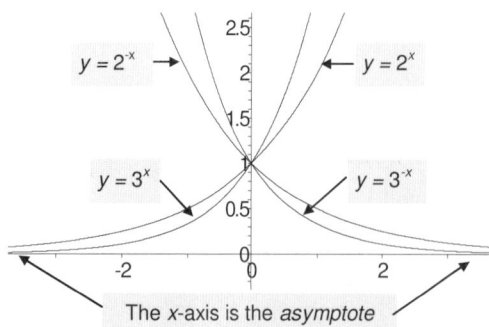

The x-axis is the *asymptote*

Graphs: Exponential graphs are *asymptotic* – that is, they get closer and closer to a line without ever reaching it. Exponential graphs which increase are based on $y = a^x$; those which decrease are based on $y = a^{-x}$. Also, $y = a^x$ always passes through $(0, 1)$ for any value of a (because $a^0 = 1$).

Graphs of other exponential functions: The graph of $y = ka^x$ is the same as $y = a^x$ but stretched by k in the y direction. Key features are:

- x-axis is the asymptote
- y-intercept is $(0, k)$
- graph is steeper than $y = a^x$

The graph of $y = a^x + c$ is the same as $y = a^x$ but moved upwards by a distance c. Key features are:

- $x = c$ is the asymptote
- y-intercept is $(0, c)$
- graph is parallel to $y = a^x$

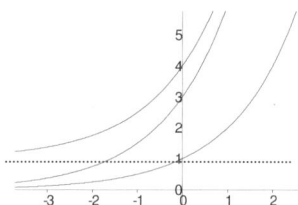

The graphs on the left are: $y = 2^x$, $y = 3 \times 2^x$, $y = 3 \times 2^x + 1$; work out which is which.

YOU SOLVE

Complete the table of values for the exponential function $y = 4^x$. For this function, find the value of x when $f(x) = 65536$.

x	0	1	2	3	4
f(x)			16	64	

To answer the second part, use your calculator to find what power of 4 gives 65536.

1, 4, 256 $x = 8$

The graph of $y = a^{kx}$ is very similar to $y = a^x$. If $k > 1$, the graph is steeper, if $k < 1$ it is less steep. Otherwise it has the same asymptote and y-intercept as $y = a^x$.

YOU SOLVE

A hot liquid is placed in a container and is allowed to cool. It's temperature, T, at a time t minutes later is given by $T = 15 + 20 \times 3^{-0.1t}$. Draw a graph of T for $0 \leq t \leq 30$ and calculate its temperature when after 6 minutes.

You could use your GDC, but it is quite hard to get the correct scaling. Work out a couple of points.

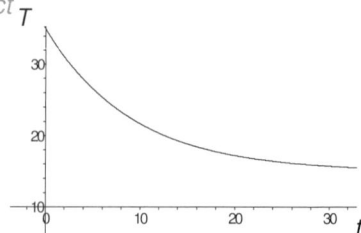

When $t = 6$, $T = $ **25.3.**

Functions and Graphs with a GDC

In this section of the syllabus, perhaps more than any other, you are expected to be able to use your graphic calculator for a wide range of techniques. You will use the calculator in four ways:

- As a simple "scientific" calculator (ie to do calculations)
- To check answers to questions you have worked out "by hand"
- To work out answers more quickly (especially for graphical questions)
- To answer questions which cannot be done in any other way

Functions: You should be able to use function keys with confidence. Make sure you know how to key in these functions:

Function	Examples
Squaring and other powers	3.2^2, 5.18^4, $(-3)^5$, -3^5
Square roots and other roots	$\sqrt{3.8}$, $\sqrt[4]{28}$
Trigonometric functions (Make sure your calculator is set in degrees)	$\sin 33^\circ$, $\cos^{-1} 0.867$

You also need to know how to use these keys to type in a function of x, eg: $y = \sqrt[3]{\dfrac{x}{x-1}}$

Tables: GDCs have a facility to work out a table of values for a function. Having input the function in the form $y = f(x)$ you can set up a table by selecting the first x value and then the steps by which you want x to increase. In this example, the function $y = 2 - 3\sin x$ has been entered into the function editor, and then a table created starting with $x = 0$ and increasing x in steps of 30. This can be helpful if you need to know several values, if you want to plot a graph by hand or if you're having difficulty creating the appropriate scales for a calculator plot – the table indicates the lowest and highest values of y.

X	Y1	
0	2	
30	.5	
60	-.5981	
90	-1	
120	-.5981	
150	.5	
180	2	

X=0

Drawing graphs: Three important points to remember when drawing and using GDC graphs.

- Make sure the function you type into the editor is actually the same as in the question. You may, for example, have to use brackets which aren't actually required on the written page. 2^{x+3}, if typed as 2 ^ x + 3, will work out values of $2^x + 3$. You need a bracket: 2 ^ (x + 3)
- The GDC has a few standard sets of scales, but you will probably have to set up the "window" yourself in order to see the required part of the graph. You may well have to zoom into a part of the graph to see exactly what is happening. The two screenshots on the right are of the same graph, but only the lower one shows the intersections with the x-axis.

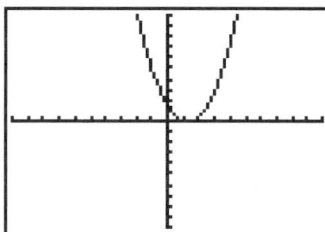

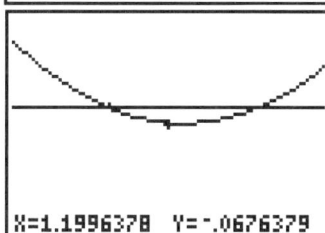

X=1.1996378 Y=-.0676379

Page 31

- The GDC can give you the values of key points such as intersections with the axes, points where lines intersect, turning points and so on. If you want to read off your own point, make sure you know the scales being used, ie how much each mark on the axes is worth.

Vertical asymptotes: A graph such as $y = 2^x$ has a horizontal asymptote because as x gets smaller, the values of y get ever closer to 0 without ever reaching it. Some functions have graphs with vertical asymptotes which arise because division by 0 is impossible. For example, $y = \dfrac{x}{x-2}$ (left) will have a vertical asymptote at $x = 2$; as x gets closer to 2, the bottom line gets closer to 0.

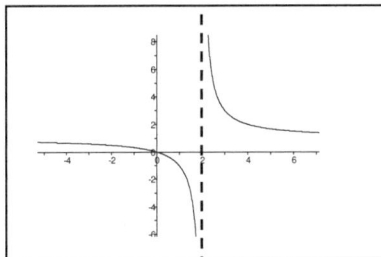

This graph also has a horizontal asymptote at $y = 1$. Note that some calculators draw vertical asymptotes in because they join all the points – but the asymptote is not part of the graph.

Solving equations: GDCs have built in equation solvers. They can sometimes be a little cumbersome to use, so it is probably better to use graphs to solve equations. The easiest way to do this is to ensure your equation has a 0 on the right hand side because then all you have to do is find out where the graph cuts the axis.

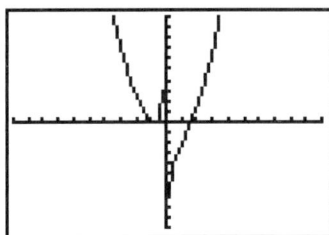

For example, solve $x^2 - 2 = \dfrac{1}{x}$, $x > 0$.

First we need to rewrite this equation as $x^2 - 2 - \dfrac{1}{x} = 0$. The graph is shown on the left.

Now use the "zero" or "root" feature to find where the graph cuts the x-axis and this will be the solution to the equation. $x = 1.618$

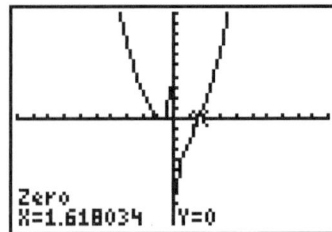

Zero
X=1.618034   Y=0

$f(x) = x^3 \times 2^{-x}$, $x \geq 0$.

a) **Sketch the graph of f(x), showing its asymptotic behaviour.**
   Note the domain of the function.

b) **Find the co-ordinates of the maximum point, and hence state the range of f(x).**
   Once you know the y-coordinate of the maximum, you can use this to write down the range; ie the set of possible values of the function. Again, note the domain.

c) **Draw a line on your graph to show that f(x) = 1 has two solutions.**

d) **Find the solutions to f(x) = 1, giving your answers to 3 significant figures.**
   Either draw y = 1 on your calculator and find the two points of intersection, or draw the graph of $y = x^3 \times 2^{-x} - 1$ and find where it intersects the x axis.

Maximum = (4.33, 4.04), Range is $0 \leq f(x) \leq 4.04$, $x = 1.37$ or 9.94

GEOMETRY AND TRIGONOMETRY

Coordinate Geometry

2-D coordinates: In 2 dimensions, we are dealing with the familiar x-y coordinate system: a pair of coordinates such as (2, 5) gives the position of a point compared to the origin (0, 0).

If you can't remember which is x and which is y, remember that the order of the coordinates is "along the corridor, up the stairs" (but not much use if you live in a bungalow).

Formulae

The gradient betweenFor two points (x_1, y_1) and (x_2, y_2):

Midpoint formula is:

$$\left(\frac{x_1 + x_2}{2}, \frac{y_1 + y_2}{2} \right)$$

Distance between the points is:

$$\sqrt{(x_2 - x_1)^2 + (y_2 - y_1)^2}$$

Gradient is:can be calculated as

$$\frac{y_2 - y_1}{x_2 - x_1}$$

Parallel lines: $m_1 = m_2$
Perpendicular lines:

Midpoint of two points:
The x coordinate of the midpoint is halfway between the x coordinates of the two points, and the y coordinate is halfway between the two y coordinates. For example, the midpoint of the line joining (-3, 6) to (5, 2) is (1, 4).

Distance between points: Because a right angled triangle can be formed with the points at two corners, we can use Pythagoras' theorem to calculate the distance. In the example shown right, the x distance between the points is 8 (from –3 to 5) and the y distance is 4 (from 2 to 6): this gives the distance between them as $\sqrt{(4^2 + 8^2)} = \sqrt{80}$.

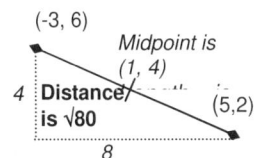

Gradient: The *gradient* of the line is its "steepness." A gradient of 3 means that y is increasing 3 times faster than x. The gradient is calculated by choosing two points and dividing the change in y by the change in x.

Horizontal lines have gradient 0. Vertical lines have an infinite gradient. Lines angled from bottom left to top right have positive gradients, others have negative gradients.

If two lines have gradients m_1 and m_2 then they are parallel if the gradients are equal, perpendicular if $m_1 m_2 = -1$.

Formulae: The various formulae are shown above. They are very similar and so can be quite confusing. It is often better to draw a sketch and work from that.

An object moving in a straight line passes through the points (3, 0) and (2, 3). the object also passes through the point (0, a). Calculate the value of a.

First of all, a rough diagram helps us to see what is happening.
One way to do this problem is to consider the gradient of the line.
From (3, 0) to (2, 3) is back 1, up 3. This pattern will continue up the line. The next point will be back 1, up 3, and that takes us to (1, 6). Do it again, and we get to (0, 9)
So, _$a = 9$_

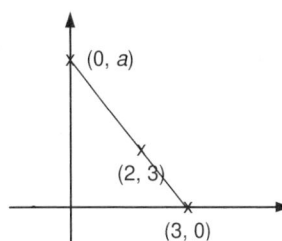

Alternatively, work out the equation of the line, and find y when $x = 0$

3-D coordinates: The 2-D coordinate system can be easily extended to define the positions of points in 3 dimensional space. Imagine the usual *x-y* axes laid flat on the floor, and a third axis – the *z* axis – drawn vertically upwards from the origin. Three coordinates in the form (*x, y, z*) are now used for the positions of points.

However, diagrams are now much harder to draw, and you will not be expected to do so, except for the simplest points. Sometimes a three axis diagram is drawn for you, and the convention is that you look *into* the origin from a point somewhere above the first quadrant of the *xy* plane (although other views are sometimes used):

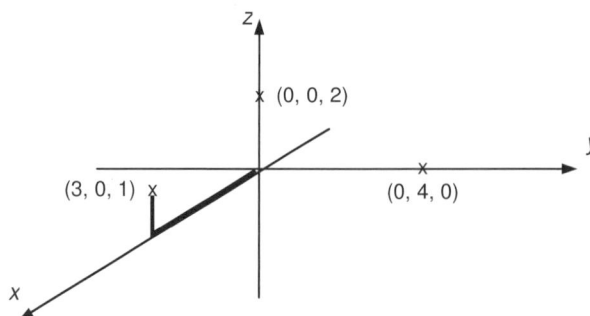

Midpoint and distance between points: The methods for finding the midpoint of two points and the distance between two points are very similar to those for 2 dimensions. For the midpoint, we find the halfway values (ie the means) for all three coordinates. For example, the midpoint of (2, 0, -4) and (5, -2, 6) is (3.5, -1, 1). The formula for the midpoint of (x_1, y_1, z_1) and (x_2, y_2, z_2) is:

$$\left(\frac{x_1 + x_2}{2}, \frac{y_1 + y_2}{2}, \frac{z_1 + z_2}{2} \right)$$

Instead of using the formula, you can calculate "informally" (eg: by saying "what number is halfway between 2 and 5" and so on)

The distance between two points is calculated using an extension of Pythagoras' theorem. For the same two points, the formula is:

$$\sqrt{(x_2 - x_1)^2 + (y_2 - y_1)^2 + (z_2 - z_1)^2}$$

For example, the distance from (5, -1, 3) to (2, -4, 4) is:

$$\sqrt{(2-5)^2 + (-4-(-1))^2 + (4-3)^2} = \sqrt{9+9+1} = \sqrt{19}$$

You must be very careful (as ever) with minus signs: in the sum above for example, we have -4 – (-1). This is -4 + 1 = -3. In other words, the distance from -1 to -4 is -3. When squared, this gives us +9 (you will never get any minuses in the final expression).

YOU SOLVE

a)On the grid, plot the points A(4, 2, 0), B(0, 3, 1) and C(0, 0, 5). Join ABC to form a triangle and calculate the length of side AB.
(Note that the axes are shown differently to the convention above).

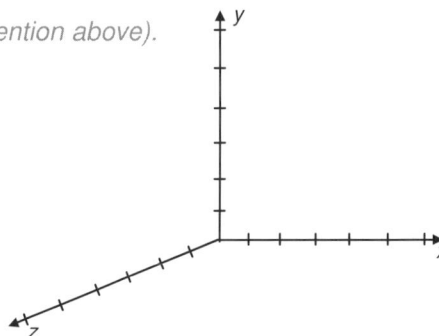

AB = √18
(A question like this could then continue to use, say, the cosine rule. A triangle is a triangle, whether in 2 or 3 dimensions).

Solution of Triangles

Right-angled triangles: This page is a reminder of how to deal with the sides and angles of a right-angled triangle. The following page deals with non right-angled triangles.

Pythagoras' Theorem: If you know two sides of a right-angled triangle, you can calculate the third using Pythagoras' Theorem. This states that the square of the hypotenuse (the longest side) equals the sum of the squares of the two shorter sides. As applied to the triangle on the right, $c^2 = a^2 + b^2$. You must remember to subtract if you already have the hypotenuse (it's always opposite the right angle) and want to calculate one of the other sides. For example, $b^2 = c^2 - a^2$.

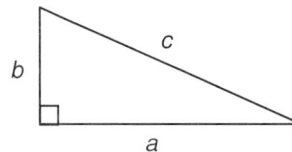

Trigonometry: There is no mystery to sin, cos and tan. They simply represent the ratios of pairs of sides for a triangle with given angles. For example, suppose the smallest angle in the triangle above right is 30°. Whatever the *size* of the triangle, *b* turns out to be half of *c*. The ratio of *b* to *c* is called the sine (sin for short), so sin30° = 0.5. The ratio of *a* to *c* is called the cosine (cos), and *b* to *a* is the tangent (tan). If you use the following procedure *in all cases* then every question can be worked out in the same way, and you should always get the right answer.

1. Label the three sides of the triangle with H (for hypotenuse, the side opposite the right angle), O (for opposite, the side opposite the angle you are dealing with) and A (for adjacent, the side next to the angle).

2. For the two sides you are dealing with, write down the word sin, cos or tan according to the mnemonic SOH/CAH/TOA.

3. Now write down the angle (which may be unknown) followed by an equals sign.

4. On the right hand side of the equals sign, you will write down a fraction (O over H, A over H or O over A) which will either involve two known sides, or one known and one unknown side.

5. You will now have an equation to solve. The three examples below show how to do this.

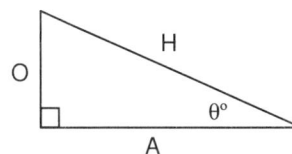

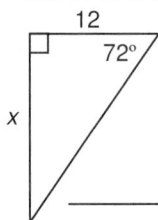

Find *x*.
x is O, 12 is A, so we use tan.
Write down tan, then the angle, then =, then the fraction O/A.
To solve this equation, just multiply through by 12.

$$\tan 72 = \frac{x}{12}$$
$$12 \times \tan 72 = x$$
$$x = 36.9$$

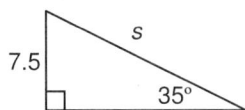

Find *s*.
s is H, 7.5 is O, so we use sin.
Write down sin, then the angle, then =, then the fraction O/H *(note that this time the unknown side will be on the bottom of the fraction).*
This time, we must "cross-multiply" to solve the equation.

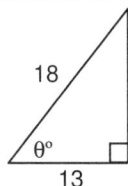

$$\sin 35 = \frac{7.5}{s}$$
$$s = \frac{7.5}{\sin 35}$$
$$s = 13.1$$

Find the angle θ°.
13 is A, 18 is H, so we use cos.
Write down cos, then the angle, then =, then the fraction A/H.
Calculate the value of the fraction, then use the cos[-1] function to find out the angle (cos[-1] means "find the angle whose cosine is...)

$$\cos \theta = \frac{13}{18}$$
$$\cos \theta = 0.7222$$
$$\theta = \cos^{-1} 0.7222$$
$$\theta = 43.8°$$

▦ Having worked out 13/18, leave the answer on the display. Then work out the angle using cos[-1]ANS. This ensures full accuracy.

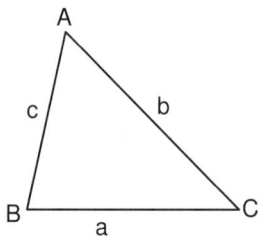

Sine and Cosine Rules: For triangles which are *not* right-angled we use the sine and cosine rules. The triangle on the left has the conventional notation of small letters for the lengths of sides and capital letters for the angles opposite. To find lengths and angles, use:

- The sine rule if 2 sides and 2 angles are involved
- The cosine rule if 3 sides and 1 angle are involved

📋 It is perhaps worth having programs for the two forms of the cosine rule, but the sine rule is very easy to use.

SINE RULE	COSINE RULE
$\dfrac{a}{\sin A} = \dfrac{b}{\sin B} = \dfrac{c}{\sin C}$	$a^2 = b^2 + c^2 - 2bc\cos A$ *(for a side)* $\cos A = \dfrac{b^2 + c^2 - a^2}{2bc}$ *(for an angle)*

Don't be put off by the letters. Basically, the sine rule says the ratio of side/sine is the same for each pair of sides and angles. And in the cosine rule, ensure that the side on the LHS of the equation matches the angle on the RHS.

In triangle ABC, angle B = 43°, AC = 6.8 cm and AB = 4.3cm. Find the size of angle A, giving your answer to the nearest degree.

It is essential to draw a rough diagram which will show you how to proceed.
We know 2 sides and 1 angle and we want another angle, so we use
the sine rule. We can only find angle C at the moment, using:

$\dfrac{4.3}{\sin C} = \dfrac{6.8}{\sin 43}$ which gives C = 25.55°. So A = 180 – (43+25.55)

A = 111.45° = 111° to the nearest degree

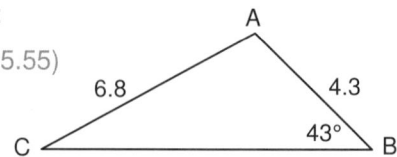

YOU SOLVE

Town A is 48km from town B and 32km from town C. If B is 56km from town C, find the size of angle CAB to the nearest degree.

Use the cosine rule (in its second form), making sure that the side opposite angle A is also on the left hand side of the formula.

CAB = 86°

Area of a non-right angled triangle: If you know two sides of a triangle, and the size of the angle between the two sides, then the area of the triangle can be found using:

☐ Area = $\dfrac{1}{2}ab\sin C$

The diagram shows a triangle with sides 5, 7 and 8. Find the size of the smallest angle and the area of the triangle.

The smallest angle is opposite the smallest side, 5.

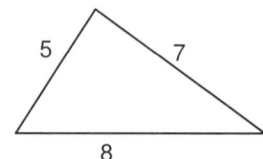

$\cos x = \dfrac{7^2 + 8^2 - 5^2}{2 \times 7 \times 8} = 0.786$. So the angle is **38.2°**

Area = ½ × 7 × 8 × sin38.2° = **17.3**
(Remember that the angle used in the area formula must be between the two sides used).

Bearings: One of the practical applications of non-right angled trigonometry is the calculation of distances and angles for moving ships and planes. Their direction of travel is based on compass directions, called *bearings*. A bearing is an angle measured around clockwise from North. Always draw in North lines on your diagrams before marking in bearings.

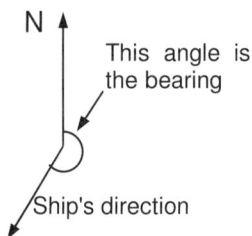

N

This angle is the bearing

Ship's direction

If a question involves bearings between places, check whether you are dealing with the bearing of A from B or the bearing from A to B, which is the other way round. Use arrows to show in which direction to take the bearing, and put the North line at the *start* of the arrow.

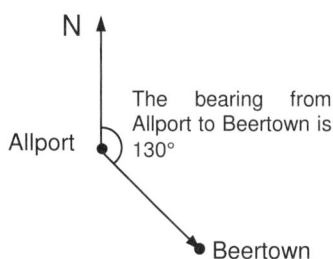

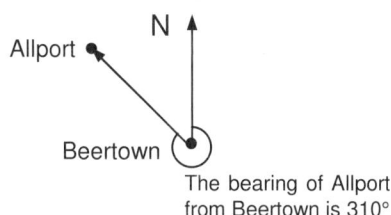

N

Allport

The bearing from Allport to Beertown is 130°

Beertown

N

Allport

Beertown

The bearing of Allport from Beertown is 310°

There is always a difference of 180° between bearings in opposite directions.

A ship sails from port P and travels due South to port Q. From port Q it sails on a bearing of 065° and travels for 45km to a point R, which is due East of P.
a) i) Draw and label clearly a diagram to show P, Q and R.
ii) Calculate the distance form port P to point R.

In questions like this the diagram is an important tool, so make it large. Angles do not have to be accurate nor lengths drawn to scale, but make them look approximately right.

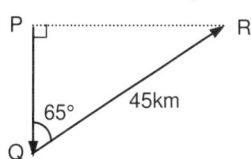

P   R

65°   45km

Q

ii) Using SOHCAHTOA (because the triangle is right angled) we can see that $\sin 65 = \dfrac{PR}{45} \Rightarrow PR = 45\sin 65 = 40.8$

The distance from P to R is 40.8km

A second ship also sails from port P for 45km to a point S, but on a bearing of 330°.
b) Complete your diagram in part (a) to show point S.
c) Calculate the distance from R to S (shown with a grey dotted line) and the angle PRS.

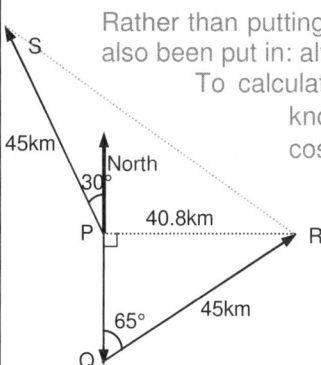

Rather than putting in 330°, the more useful 30° has been shown instead. The 40.8 has also been put in: always keep your diagrams up-to-date with new information.

S

45km

North

30°

P   40.8km   R

65°   45km

Q

To calculate RS, we use triangle PRS which is not right angled. We already know two sides and one angle (SPR = 30 + 90 = 120°), so we use the cosine rule: $RS^2 = 45^2 + 40.783^2 - 2 \times 45 \times 40.783 \times \cos 120$

RS = √5523.6 = 74.3km (Check: RS < RP + PS. Looks OK)
Now we need to calculate angle PRS. We know one angle and two sides so we use the sine rule.

$\dfrac{\sin PRS}{45} = \dfrac{\sin 120}{74.321} \Rightarrow \sin PRS = \dfrac{45\sin 120}{74.321} = 0.5244$

So angle PRS = sin⁻¹(0.5244) = 31.6°

d) What is the bearing of S from R?

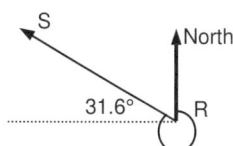

S

North

31.6°   R

The diagram shows the arrow representing S from R, and a new North line inserted. The required bearing has also been put in. How big is this angle? From North round to West is 270°, and then we need another 31.6. So, **the bearing of S from R = 301.6°**
(Note that throughout the question calculations have been performed with numbers to 4 SF accuracy, even if answers are given to 3 SF)

3-D Geometry

You have to be able to combine the rules of 3-D coordinates with the trigonometry of both right angled and non-right angled triangles in order to find the sides and angles of cuboids, prisms and pyramids.

Cuboid: A cuboid is the 3-D equivalent of a rectangle. It has 12 sides, 4 each in three different dimensions (the length, width and height). Commonly asked questions involve the lengths of diagonals (both of sides and also of from one corner to the opposite corner) and angles between various lines. The points used will be the vertices (corners) and the midpoints of sides.

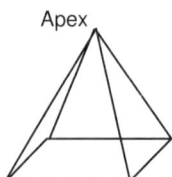

Pyramid: You only have to concern yourself with a "right" pyramid – ie where the apex is directly above the centre of the base, which is itself a square. Pyramid questions almost invariably use the midpoints of sides, and it should be noted that a line drawn from the midpoint of one of the base edges to the apex is at right angles to the base edge.

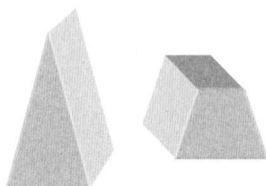

Prism: A prism is any 3-D shape with the same cross-section throughout its length. Very often this cross-section is a triangle, but it does not have to be.

Angle between a line and a plane: A plane is a flat surface, so each of the faces of the 3-D shapes on the left is a plane. The angle between a line and a plane is the angle between the line and its *projection* on the plane: think of the projection as part of a "shadow line" on the plane.

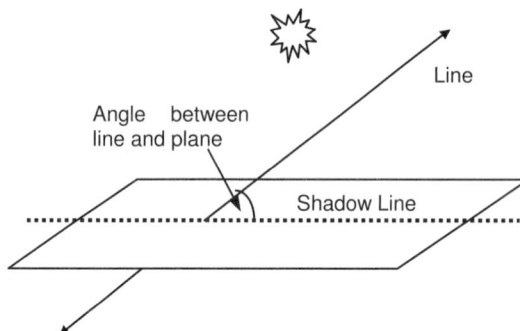

Calculating lengths and angles in 3 dimensions: Basically, you convert each question into an appropriate 2-D question, usually by identifying a right-angled triangle containing the length/angle you have to work out, drawing it as it really looks, then using trigonometry and Pythagoras as usual. For example, the base edges of a pyramid are 10cm and the slant edges are 12cm. M is the midpoint of side PQ and X is the centre point of the base. Find length AM and angle AMX to the nearest degree.

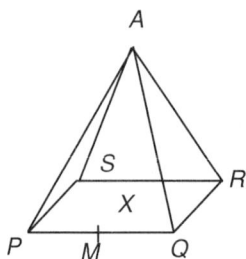

We can find AM using triangle AMQ. MQ = 5 (half of the base length) so $AM^2 = 12^2 - 5^2 \Rightarrow$ AM = $\sqrt{119}$. Now we can draw triangle AMX because we know MX = 5 and AM = $\sqrt{119}$. We can see from the diagram on the left that $\cos AMX = \dfrac{5}{\sqrt{119}} = 0.458$, so angle AMX = 63°,

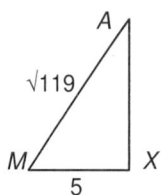

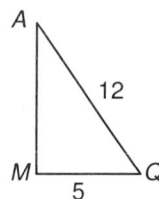

Here is a complete worked paper 2 question:

An office tower is in the shape of a cuboid with a square base. The roof of the tower is in the shape of a square based right pyramid. The diagram shows some dimensions but is not to scale.

a)   Calculate, correct to 3 significant figures:

   i)   The angle between OF and FG;

   ii)   The shortest distance from O to FG;

   iii)   The total surface area of the four triangular roof sections.

   iv)   The size of the angle between the slant height of the roof and the plane EFGH;

   v)   The height of the tower from the base to O.

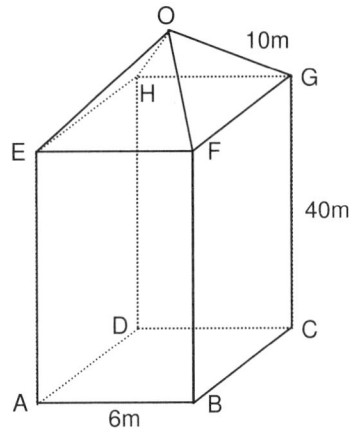

i) Since the pyramid is symmetrical, all the slant heights are 10m. The length FG is 6m because it is the same as AB. We draw triangle OFG, and can use the trigonometry of an isosceles triangle.

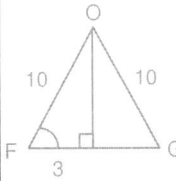

$$\cos OFG = \frac{3}{10} = 0.3 \Rightarrow \underline{\textbf{OFG = 72.5°}}$$

ii)   The shortest distance from O to FG can also be seen in the same triangle – it is the line straight down from O to the midpoint of the base – call it X. We could use trigonometry or Pythagoras. $OX^2 + 3^2 = 10^2 \Rightarrow \underline{\textbf{OX = }\sqrt{91}}$

iii) Looking at the diagram for triangle OFG, we can see that its base is 6m and its height has just been calculated as $\sqrt{91}$m. So the area of the triangle is $0.5 \times 6 \times \sqrt{91} = 28.62m^2$
So the total area of the roof $= 28.62 \times 4 = \underline{\textbf{114.5m}^2}$

iv)   Imagine the shadow line of OF on the plane EFGH – it is along the line FH. So we need the angle between OF and FH. FH would be a useful length to know: using Pythagoras on triangle FGH we get $FH^2 = 6^2 + 6^2 \Rightarrow FH = \sqrt{72}$. Is there a right angled triangle we could use to find angle OFH? Yes, if we drop a line from O to the centre of the base of the pyramid: call this point P. FP is half the diagonal FH ie $0.5 \times \sqrt{72}$. Now we can easily calculate OFP

$$\cos OFP = \frac{0.5 \times \sqrt{72}}{10} = 0.424 \Rightarrow \underline{\textbf{OFP = 65°}}$$

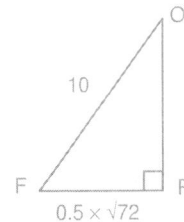

v) The height of the tower will be the height of the cuboid + OP
Height of tower $= 40 + 10\sin65 = \underline{\textbf{49.1m}}$

b)   A parrot's nest is perched at a point, P, on the edge of BF of the tower. A person at point A, outside the building, measures the angle of elevation to point P to be 79°. Find, correct to 3 significant figures, the height of the nest from the base of the tower.

We need to draw triangle ABF with the point P marked on it.
Now we can see that the distance we require is BP, and we can use right angled triangle ABP.

$$\tan79° = \frac{BP}{6} \Rightarrow BP = 6\tan79° = \underline{\textbf{30.9m}}$$

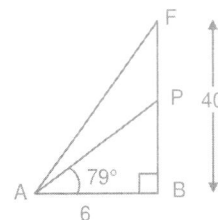

Cylinder, Sphere and Cone

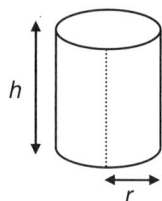

Curved Surface Area: Whilst the concept of the *volume* of shapes with curved edges and faces may not be too difficult to appreciate, the *area* of such curved faces may be problematic. The way to think of such faces is to imagine them to be made from separate pieces of paper; the area of a curved surface is the same as the area of the paper it is made from when it is flattened out. For example, unroll the curved surface of a cylinder and you get a rectangle whose height is the height of the cylinder and whose length is the circumference of the cylinder.

Cut along the dotted line and open up to get...

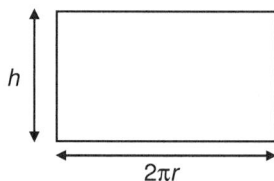

You need to be able to use the relevant area and volume formulae for cylinders, cones and spheres. You will find them all in your list of formulae.They are:

Cylinder: Curved surface area = $2\pi rh$
Volume = $\pi r^2 h$

Cone: Curved surface area = πrl (*l* is the slant height)
Volume = $\frac{1}{3}\pi r^2 h$

Sphere: Surface area = $4\pi r^2$
Volume = $\frac{4}{3}\pi r^3$

Read each question very carefully to see *exactly* what you are being asked to find. For example, a cylinder may be completely closed in which case the total surface area is the curved surface area plus the areas of the two end, which are both circles. Or it may be open at one end, so just add one circle. The volume of a hemisphere is half that of a sphere, but its total surface area will be half the curved surface of a sphere plus the circle which forms its base. Its formula will be $\frac{1}{2}\times 4\pi r^2 + \pi r^2 = 3\pi r^2$.

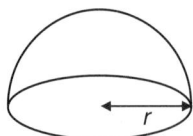

Both a cone and a hemisphere have base diameter of 18cm. If the height of the cone is 10cm, show that the ratio of the volume of the cone to that of the hemisphere is 5:9.

The volume of the cone is $\frac{1}{3}\pi r^2 h = \frac{1}{3}\pi \times 9^2 \times 10 = 270\pi$. The volume of the hemisphere is

$\frac{1}{2}\times\frac{4}{3}\pi r^3 = \frac{2}{3}\pi \times 9^3 = 486\pi$. Two things to note. Firstly, the question specified diameter, but we

must use the radius – an old trap! Secondly, we keep π in the answer so as to keep the values exact.

So. volume of cone:volume of hemisphere = $270\pi:486\pi = 5\pi:9\pi$ = **5:9**

YOU SOLVE

The diagram shows a cone on top of a cylinder. Find the surface area and the volume.
The circle at the base of the cone will not form part of the surface area since it is inside the shape. You will need Pythagoras' Theorem to calculate the slant height of the cone.

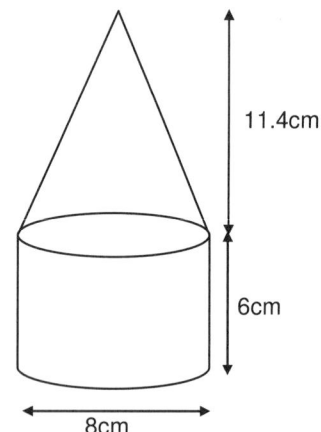

11.4cm

6cm

8cm

<u>A = 353cm^2</u>, <u>V = 493cm^3</u>

STATISTICS

Basics of Statistics

Definitions: A *population* is a set from which *statistics* are drawn. A *sample* is a subset drawn from the population. Sample statistics (such as the mean) can be used to estimate population statistics. *Discrete* data are restricted to certain values only (often integers) whereas *continuous* data can take any values. The *frequency* is the number of times a particular value occurs. A *frequency table* shows how often each value occurs in a discrete distribution. In a continuous distribution, it is necessary to use a *grouped* frequency table. Numerical data is usually collected into a table and then split into *groups* or *classes*. The *boundaries* of the classes must be dealt with carefully, especially for continuous data. Consider a table of weights (see right): into which class would a weight of 10kg be put? It would be better if the first group were labelled as $0 \leq w < 10$ and the second as $10 \leq w < 20$ and then 10 would fall into the second group. The *interval width* in this case is 10, and the *mid-interval value* of the first group is 5 and so on.

Examples of populations:
People who live in Europe
People who drive
Apples grown in France
Cars made in 2001

Examples of discrete data:
Shoe sizes
Goals scored by a team
Number of chocolates in a box

Examples of continuous data
Weights of people
Athletes' times to run 100m
Heights of mountains

Weight (kg)
0 – 10
10 - 20

Frequency Diagrams: Data can be appreciated more when displayed in a diagram. *Frequency polygons* are a simple way of displaying discrete data; for grouped data, *frequency histograms* (bar charts) are very easy to construct. A frequency histogram uses equal class intervals. If the data is continuous, there cannot be gaps between the bars.

This table lists the heights of 55 children:

131	136	142	145	153	144	140	145	137	136	140
133	133	146	144	138	134	142	142	149	147	136
152	148	142	143	144	134	134	147	141	139	144
135	135	150	137	132	139	141	149	131	148	136
132	137	138	143	142	140	150	149	145	147	144

The frequency table and frequency histogram are shown below:

Height h (cm)	Frequency
$130 < h \leq 135$	10
$135 < h \leq 140$	15
$140 < h \leq 145$	17
$145 < h \leq 150$	11
$150 < h \leq 155$	2
Total	55

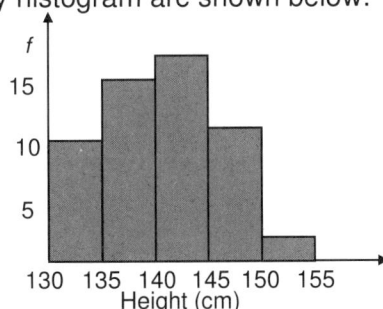

It is also possible to draw a *frequency polygon* to represent the data. This is a line graph which joins up the midpoints of the tops of the bars.

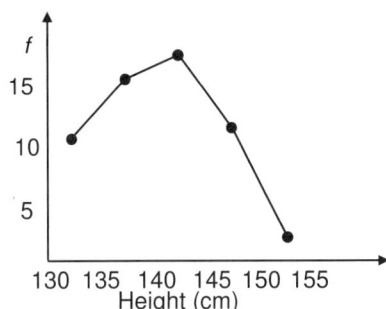

Stem and Leaf Diagrams: One of the drawbacks of a histogram is that the original data values are lost when they are grouped together. A stem and leaf diagram (stem plot) displays the original data in a form which has some of the properties of a histogram. The stem plot below shows the lengths of 40 leaves collected from a tree:

```
4 | 1  4  6  7
5 | 0  2  2  5  6  9
6 | 1  1  3  6  6  8  9  9
7 | 0  0  1  2  3  5  5  5  7  8
8 | 1  3  4  6  7
9 | 0  0  2  4  4  6  6
```

There needs to be a key. For example, 6|3 represents 6.3cm. Note that the data has been sorted and, since data values are lined up in columns, the length of the row is equivalent to the height of a bar in a histogram. It is simple to read off the mode and median (see page 43) from a stem plot.

A new fertiliser was applied to 20 fruit bushes to see if their yield of fruit increased. Another 20 trees were left untreated. The yields, in kg, were as follows:

Treated	Untreated
22 37 41 55 52	20 37 37 50 12
19 32 39 44 40	26 21 46 31 49
50 28 44 38 24	13 21 40 18 28
40 31 43 47 54	26 39 24 33 48

Construct a sorted stem and leaf diagram to compare the two sets of data and comment on the effects of the new fertiliser.

```
        Untreated                         Treated

              8  3  2 | 1 | 9
     8  6  6  4  1  1  0 | 2 | 2  4  8
           9  7  7  3  1 | 3 | 1  2  7  8  9
              9  8  6  0 | 4 | 0  0  1  3  4  4  7
                       0 | 5 | 0  2  4  5
```

1|9 = 19kg

The stem and leaf diagram shows that the treated fruit bushes generally have a higher yield. This would seem to indicate that the new fertiliser is effective.

Measures of Central Tendency: One of the most basic statistics which can be used as a figure to represent the whole group is an average. You are required to know three different averages: the *mean*, *mode* and the *median*.

Mean: To calculate the mean, add all the numbers together and divide by the number of values. If the data is in a frequency table then the total value is calculated by multiplying each value by its frequency and totalling the result. Note that the number of values is *not* the number of classes, but the sum of the frequencies.

In the table, there were a total of 19 days absence over a period of 30 days. So the

Pupils absent (x)	No of days (f)	fx
0	20	0
1	4	4
2	3	6
3	3	9
TOTAL	30	19

mean number of days absent was 19/30 = 0.63 (It is a common mistake to divide 19 by 4, the number of classes).

If the data is presented in a grouped frequency table, the same procedure is followed except that the mid-interval value of each group is used to represent the *x* value for each group. This means that the *actual* data values are unknown and in this case the mean is only an estimate. "Calculate an estimate of the mean" does *not* mean that you make a guess!

Weight of apples (*w*)	No of apples (*f*)	Mid interval	*fx*
20 ≤ *w* < 25	12	22.5	270
25 ≤ *w* < 30	20	27.5	550
30 ≤ *w* < 35	25	32.5	812.5
35 ≤ *w* < 40	17	37.5	637.5
TOTAL	74		**2270**

Estimated mean weight of an apple is $\frac{2270}{74} = 30.7g$

Always check if the answer is "reasonable." Look at the distribution of weights – does 30.7 look like the mean?

Mode: The mode is the value that occurs most often. In a frequency table, it is the value with the highest frequency. In a grouped frequency table, the best you can do is say which *class* has the highest frequency – this is called the *modal class* or *modal group*. The modal class above is 30 ≤ *w* < 35 g.

Median: If a set of values is listed in ascending order, the middle value is the *median*. It is another type of average: there are as many values above the median as below it. Unlike the mean, it is unaffected by extra large or extra small values. In the following list there are 15 values so the 8th is the middle one (7 below it, 7 above it.

   1 1 3 5 6 6 6 **7** 7 9 10 10 12 15 18   Median = 7

If there are an even number of values, find the mean of the middle two to calculate the median.

   24 26 27 **27 29** 30 30 33   Median = 28

Go back to the stem plot at the top of page 42. Show that the mode is 7.5 and the median is 7.05.

For the set of marks {7, 4, 2, 11, 2, 5, 10, 12, 2, 5}
a)   Calculate the mean;

b)   Find the mode;

c)   Find the median. *(Remember to put them in order first).*

YOU SOLVE

6,   2,   5

The annual salaries of employees in a company are given in the table.

Category (*x*)	Number of employees (*f*)	Salary	*fx*
Trainees	8	£4000	32000
Computer Operators	6	£10100	60600
Secretaries	8	£13500	108000
Salesmen	9	£21000	189000
Managers	3	£26000	78000
TOTALS	34		467600

a)   What is the modal salary?
b)   Calculate the mean salary to 2 decimal places.

(The original table had the first three columns. I have added the fourth and the totals row).
a)   Modal salary is £21000 since more people earn it than any other.
b)   Mean salary = 467600 ÷34 = **£13753**

Cumulative Frequency

Cumulative frequency tables: It is slightly easier to calculate the median from a frequency table if it is first converted into a *cumulative frequency table.* Whether the data is discrete or continuous, the method is the same. Each value of cumulative frequency measures how many x values there are in total up to that point. Consider the following grouped frequency table:

This table uses the convention that 0 – means "from 0 up to the next value" (5 in this case).

x	0 -	5 -	10 -	15 -	20 -	25 - 30
f	4	11	17	25	14	4

If we now find the number of x values *up to* the top value in each group, we get the following cumulative frequency table:

Note that in the conversion of the grouped frequency table, the "up to" points are the **top** of each group

x	<5	<10	<15	<20	<25	<30
c. f.	4	15	32	57	71	75

Now we plot the points (5, 4), (10, 15) and so on.

The points in the table are plotted and are joined either by straight lines or a smooth curve. To find the median, a line is drawn to the right from 38 (the middle value of the distribution) and down to the x axis. The median can be seen to be about 16.

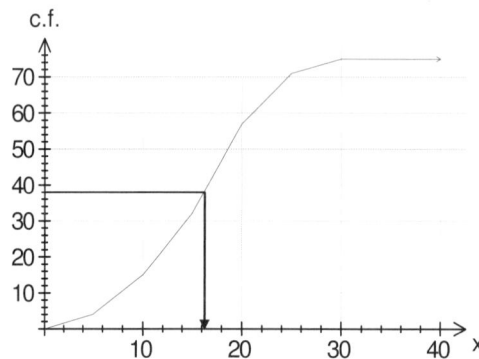

Quartiles: 50% of the population lie above the median, 50% below. We can also divide the population into *quartiles*: 25% lie below the first quartile, 50% below the second (which is also the median) 75% below the third quartile. There are 75 results in the previous table, so the first quartile will be the 19th result (19 is about one quarter of 75). Looking at the graph, this gives the first quartile as 11 and the third quartile (the 57th result) as 20. Similarly, the distribution can be divided into 100 parts knows as *percentile.* "Your test result is in the top 5 percentiles of the population" means that at least 95% of people scored worse than you did.

At a school athletics meeting the times for running 200m were entered in a table.

Time in seconds	26	27	28	29	30
Number of boys	7	17	16	14	6

a) **Complete the cumulative frequency table for these results.**

Time in seconds	Number of boys
<26.5	7
<27.5	
<28.5	
<29.5	
<30.5	

b) **The fastest 20% of boys qualify to enter a regional competition. Estimate the slowest qualifying time.** *(There are 60 boys. Estimate the time of the 12th boy)*

24, 40, 54, 60   26.8s

A biologist recorded as a frequency distribution the diameters (D), measured to the nearest millimetre, of 100 rose petals. The result are given in the table below.

Diameter of petal	Number of petals	Diameter of petal	Cum. frequency
$27 < L \le 29$	2	≤ 29	2
$29 < L \le 31$	4	≤ 31	6
$31 < L \le 33$	8	≤ 33	14
$33 < L \le 35$	21	≤ 35	35
$35 < L \le 37$	30	≤ 37	65
$37 < L \le 39$	18	≤ 39	83
$39 < L \le 41$	12	≤ 41	95
$41 < L \le 43$	5	≤ 43	100
	100		

a) **Construct a cumulative frequency table for the data.** (Completed in grey).
b) **Draw a cumulative frequency curve and use it to estimate the median, the lower and upper quartiles.**

a) Draw a line over from 50 on the *y*-axis to the graph then down to the *x*-axis. This will be the median.
Median = 36cm

b) For the quartiles, do the same as for the median, except that you take the lines from the 25 and the 75.
Lower quartile = 34cm   Upper quartile = 38
(These results are to the nearest centimetre)

Note that the construction lines do not *have* to be shown, but the examiner will like to see them.

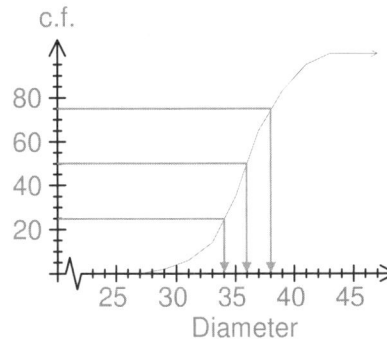

Box and Whisker Plots: Why are there so many different ways of presenting data? Because although tables and diagrams are much easier to interpret that raw data, different types of presentation allow for a variety of analyses of the data to be made. A box and whisker plot shows the following information:

- Extreme values
- Lower quartile
- Median
- Upper quartile.

The box plot for the data on treated fruit bushes (page 42) looks like this.

What information can we read from this box plot? Apart from the actual values of the quartiles and the medain, we see that the extreme values are not too far from the bulk of the values as represented by the box (the middle 50% of values). The median is slightly to the right of centre implying that there are more values towards the upper end of the distribution.

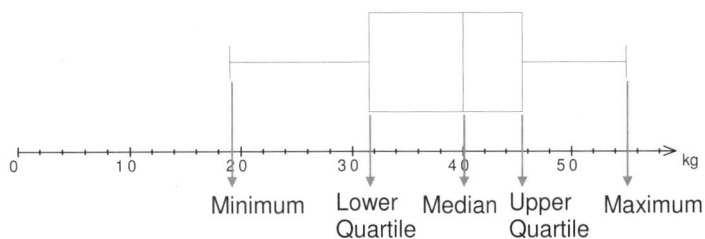

Box plots are particularly useful when set against each other. Here is the data for both treated and untreated bushes.

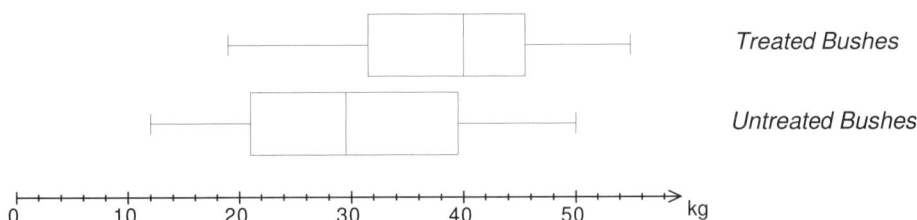

Treated Bushes

Untreated Bushes

Measures of Dispersion

The most useful summary statistics for a set of data are the "average" (mean or median; mode is not representative of all the data), and the *spread*. Such a measure gives an indication of how the data is dispersed around the average.

Range: The range is the difference between the highest and lowest values. It is a crude measure of spread since it does not take the other values into account at all.

Interquartile range: The IQR is the difference between the first and third quartiles (the 25th and 75th percentiles). This gives us the spread of the middle 50% of values, and thus leaves out possible extreme values at each end. On a box plot, the IQR is the length of the box (as measured against the scale). The box plots on the previous page give an IQR of 14 for the treated bushes, 18.5 for the untreated bushes, indicating that treated bushes give a more consistent yield. (Remember that word for exam questions).

Standard deviation: The standard deviation is, roughly, the average deviation of all the values from the mean. Unlike the IQR, which only depends on the middle 50% of values, the standard

> You can also read off the median and the quartiles from your calculator display – but not if you have input the mid-interval values of a grouped distribution.

deviation uses all the values. 🖩 You must know how to put data values into your calculator (including in the form a frequency table) and then read off the mean and standard deviation.

Try calculating the standard deviation of the weight of peanuts in these 80 packets:

You should find that the mean weight is 96.8 and the standard deviation is 7.41.

Weight	No of packets
$80 \leq W < 85$	5
$85 \leq W < 90$	10
$90 \leq W < 95$	15
$95 \leq W < 100$	26
$100 \leq W < 105$	13
$105 \leq W < 110$	7
$110 \leq W < 115$	4

> A class takes a mathematics test. The mean score is 65%, and the standard deviation is 8%. This means that most of the scores will be in the range 49% - 81%.

As a rough indicator, the majority of results in a reasonably symmetrical distribution are within two standard deviations of the mean.

> **Notation**
> μ = population mean
> σ = population standard deviation
> $\bar{X}$ = sample mean
> s = sample standard deviation
> **but** *your GDC may use different symbols.*

Population and sample statistics: Usually there are too many members in a population to be able to record *all* the values for a distribution; thus the population mean is unknown. However, if we take a large enough sample, we can use the sample mean as an estimate for the population mean. The sample standard deviation is smaller than the population standard deviation, but for the purposes of this course can be used as an estimate.

The mean number of children per female for a group of 25 women was 1.3 and the standard deviation was 1.08. For a second group of 25 the mean was 2.2 and the standard deviation 2.1. Describe the differences between the numbers of children for the two groups.

The second group has almost twice as many children per female as the first group. In addition, the dispersion is greater, indicating that some people in the second group have quite large numbers of children.

(Note: using the "two standard deviation test", the range for the first group is –0.86 to 3.46 (in practice, 0 to 3) and for the second group is –2 to 6.4 (in practice 0 to 6).

Correlation

Scatter diagrams: Two sets of data which appear to have a relationship between them are said to be *correlated*. For example, a company may find that there is a direct relationship between the amount it spends on advertising and its sales figures. Note that correlation does not imply causality: the correlation may be coincidental, or it may be linked to a third factor (perhaps, in this case, differing economic conditions). A simple way to assess possible correlation is to draw a *scatter diagram*. The two sets of data are plotted on a standard *x-y* graph (but not joined in any way). Qualitative conclusions which can be drawn about the correlation are:

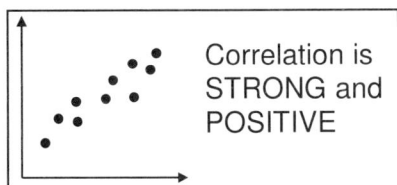

Correlation is STRONG and POSITIVE

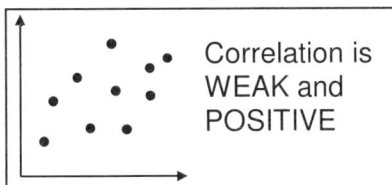

Correlation is WEAK and POSITIVE

It is not necessary for the axes in a scatter diagram to be labelled from 0. We are only interested in the relationship between the points.

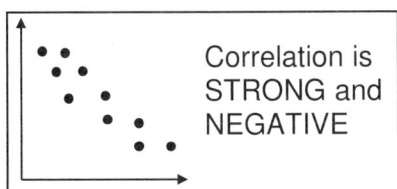

Correlation is STRONG and NEGATIVE

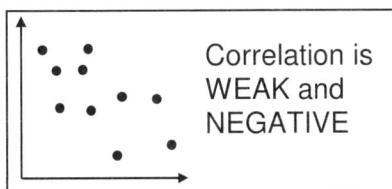

Correlation is WEAK and NEGATIVE

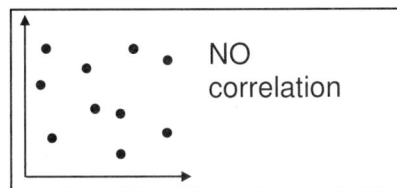

NO correlation

Note that perfect correlation (whether positive or negative) would be represented by a straight line.

Line of best fit: A scatter diagram indicates the relationship between two variables. If we conclude that there *is* a relationship, we can draw in the "line of best fit" by eye and then use this to predict more pairs of values. If you know the mean values of the two variables, the line of best fit should pass through the point $(\overline{x}, \overline{y})$. Note that although *interpolation* (ie putting new points in between existing points) is fairly safe, *extrapolation* (ie continuing the line beyond the existing points) may not be valid. There may be reasons why the relationship does not continue in the same way.

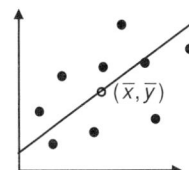

Correlation Coefficient: For a quantitative assessment of correlation we can calculate the *product-moment* coefficient, denoted by *r*. This is derived from all the pairs of values such that:
- A coefficient of −1 indicates perfect negative correlation.
- A coefficient of 0 indicates no correlation.
- A coefficient of +1 indicates perfect positive correlation.

The size of *r* (ie the positive value of *r*) indicates the strength of the correlation, but this also depends on the number of pairs of values. However, we can say generally that:
- $0.25 \leq r < 0.5 \Rightarrow$ weak correlation
- $0.5 \leq r < 0.75 \Rightarrow$ moderate correlation
- $0.75 \leq r < 1 \Rightarrow$ strong correlation

(and similarly for negative values of *r*).

Calculating the coefficient: The formula for calculating the correlation coefficient is $r = \dfrac{s_{xy}}{s_x s_y}$ where s_x and s_y are the standard deviations of the x and y values, and s_{xy} is a quantity called the *covariance* of X and Y. If the covariance is required in a question, its value will be given to you. ▣ If you are given the raw data, you can enter the numbers into your calculator and then calculate the value of r directly. You are expected to know how to do this.

YOU SOLVE

The table shows the blood pressure as measured for 9 people of varying ages.

Age	19	35	51	24	58	45	27	33	69
Blood pressure	55	60	80	65	75	85	70	75	85

Calculate the product-moment correlation coefficient and hence comment on the statement that "blood pressure increase with age."

<u>r = 0.783</u> **There is strong evidence to suggest blood pressure increases with age.**

Regression lines: The line of best fit on a scatter diagram is called a "regression line" and it can be calculated from the data pairs. The rather fearsome formula to use is:

$$y - \bar{y} = \frac{s_{xy}}{s_x^2}(x - \bar{x})$$

▣ Your calculator can be used to calculate the regression line if you have been given all the raw data.

The x and the y just sit there (you end up with the familiar straight line formula $y = ax + b$), $\bar{x}$ and $\bar{y}$ are the means of X and Y, s_{xy} is the covariance and s_x^2 is the square of the standard deviation of the x values. Let's see how this is all put together.

In a study of a city, the population density (y) was compared to the distance from the city centre (x) for a number of sample areas. The results were:

x	0.6	3.8	2.4	3.0	2.0	1.5	1.8	3.4	4.0	0.9
y	50	22	14	20	33	47	25	8	16	38

a) **Draw a scattergraph and find the equation of the regression line using the formula. You are given that $s_{xy} = -12.46$**

b) **Use your formula to predict the population density 2.2km from the centre.**

c) **Why could the regression line not be used to predict the population density 6km from the centre?**

a) We need the two means and also s_x. These can be found by entering the data into the GDC, and are as follows: $\bar{x} = 2.34, \bar{y} = 27.3, s_x = 1.125$. So the regression line formula is:

$$y - 27.3 = \frac{-12.46}{1.125^2}(x - 2.34)$$

$$y - 27.3 = -9.846(x - 2.34)$$

$$y = -9.846x + 50.3$$

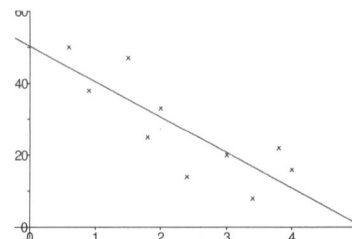

b) Substituting x into the formula gives $y = 28.7$.

c) The relationship cannot continue beyond about 5km because it would give negative values for population density.

The χ^2 Test

Contingency Tables: A contingency table is a sort of Venn Diagram which shows how a population splits according to two factors. We would like to see whether or not the two factors are independent of each other. The procedure is to take a table of observed frequencies and, from this, draw up a table of *expected* frequencies on the assumption of independence. For example, suppose we take a group of 60 people, and we are interested to find out if those who are over 21 are more likely to pass their driving test than those who are under 21. The observed frequencies are shown in the table below:

	Over 21	Under 21	Total
Pass	36	12	48
Fail	4	8	12
Total	40	20	60

Working out the expected frequencies: We can see that one-fifth of the group failed the test: we would therefore expect 8 out of the 40 over-21s to fail. 8 is the *expected* frequency, and the calculation to work it out is $\dfrac{40 \times 12}{60}$; in general, the calculation is $\dfrac{\text{row total} \times \text{column total}}{\text{grand total}}$. (Note that the numbers do not necessarily come out as integers). The table of expected frequencies is calculated as:

	Over 21	Under 21	Total
Pass	**32**	**16**	48
Fail	**8**	**4**	12
Total	40	20	60

The newly calculated figures are shown in bold

We can see that the number of over 21's who passed the test is more than we expected – could it be this high by chance alone, or could it be that the two factors (age and pass rate) are in fact related?

χ^2 **test:** We now need a statistic which measures by how much the observed frequencies differ from the expected frequencies. This is called the χ^2 statistic and is calculated as $\chi^2 = \sum \dfrac{(Obs - Exp)^2}{Exp}$. So, taking each pair of corresponding values, we have:

$$\chi^2 = \frac{(36-32)^2}{32} + \frac{(12-16)^2}{16} + \frac{(4-8)^2}{8} + \frac{(8-4)^2}{4} = 7.5$$

On its own, this doesn't tell us much. The next move is to go to a table of *critical values* which tells us at which point "could have happened by chance" becomes "unlikely to have happened by chance." The table of critical values starts like this:

Degrees of freedom	0.9	0.95	0.975	0.99
1	2.705	3.841	5.024	6.635
2	4.605	5.991	7.378	9.210
3	6.251	7.815	9.348	11.345
4	7.779	9.488	11.143	13.277
5	9.236	11.070	12.833	15.086

Find out how to enter the observed frequencies into your GDC. It can then calculate the expected frequencies and the value of χ^2.

Degrees of freedom: The more rows and columns we have, the more pairs of values there will be. So the value of χ^2 will be higher, and so will the critical value. The number of "degrees of freedom" is calculated as (rows − 1) × (columns − 1); in our example, this is $(2 − 1)(2 − 1) = 1$. The term degrees of freedom does not need to be understood, but you must be able to calculate it!

Significance level: How certain do we want to be that the value of χ^2 could not happen by chance alone? A significance level of 5% means that only in 5% of cases would you get a value this high or higher. This in turn means that if our value of χ^2 is above the critical value, we can be 95% certain that the things we are measuring *are* in fact related. If we want to be 99% certain, we go for a significance level of 1%.

The test: At the 5% level (95% certainty), and with 1 degree of freedom, we see from the table that the critical value is 3.841. Our calculated value of 7.5 > 3.841, so the differences are significant. We conclude that the test provides evidence that over-21s are more likely to pass the driving test, ie: age and pass rate are not independent.

Hypothesis testing: All of the above can be bundled up into a *hypothesis test*, and you should always write these out in the same way. We begin with a *null hypothesis* (that the quantities are independent) and an *alternative hypothesis* (that they are not independent. These are written as H_0 and H_1. Let's see how to write out the complete test:

H_0: Pass rate is independent of age
H_1: Pass rate depends on age

Significance level = 5%

$\chi^2 = 7.5$ *(see calculation above)*

Degrees of freedom = 1

Critical value = 3.841

$7.5 > 3.841 \Rightarrow$ accept H_1

Conclusion: It appears that people over 21 are more likely to pass the test.

Note that you should always finish with a conclusion that relates to actual situation – rather than just saying "accept H_1."

On the next page there is a contingency table question for you to solve. The various steps have been set up for you; you will have to carry out the calculations, look up the critical value table and decided on the conclusion.

A certain type of electronic component is made in three different factories. Samples were taken from each to see how many were defective. The contingency table below shows the results.

	Satisfactory	Defective
Factory A	90	10
Factory B	67	3
Factory C	70	10

Carry out a hypothesis test at the 5% level and decide whether the quality of the component is independent of the factory where it is made.

Write down H_0 and H_1.

Add row and column totals to the table.

	Satisfactory	Defective	Total
Factory A	90	10	
Factory B	67	3	
Factory C	70	10	
Total			

Draw up a new table with expected frequencies.

	Satisfactory	Defective	Total
Factory A			
Factory B			
Factory C			
Total			

Work out the χ^2 statistic.

Work out the number of degrees of freedom.

Look up the critical value.

Make your conclusion.

Expected frequencies are **90.8, 9.2, 63.56, 6.44, 72.64, 7.36.**

χ^2 = **3.14**, Degrees of Freedom = **2**, Critical value = **5.991**

3.14 < 5.91, **accept H_0**. No evidence to suggest quality varies between the factories.

INTRODUCTORY DIFFERENTIAL CALCULUS

Gradients of Curves

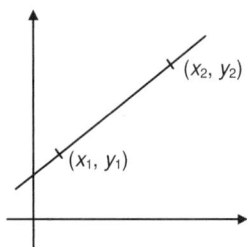

Gradient of a straight line: The gradient of the line joining two points (x_1, y_1) and (x_2, y_2) is calculated using the formula $\dfrac{y_2 - y_1}{x_2 - x_1}$.

This gives a single number which represents the rate of change of y compared to x. If the graph represents "real-life" quantities, then the gradient will have a meaning as well. Examples are:

x	y	Gradient
Time	Distance	Rate of change of distance = velocity
Time	Amount of water in a bath	Rate of increase of volume
No. of promotional brochures (in hundreds)	Cost of printing the brochures (in £)	Cost per hundred brochures

Average gradient: When a curved graph is drawn, it does not have a single value to represent gradient. But by drawing a straight line between any two points, the *average* gradient between the points can be calculated. Consider a car accelerating from rest:

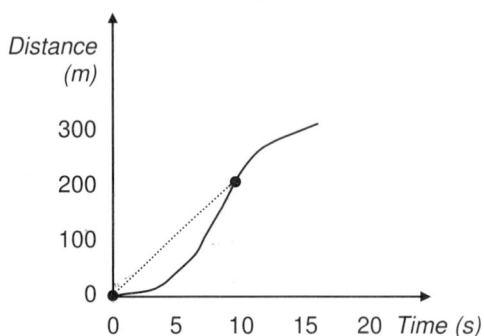

At time 0s, it is at its start position. At time 10s, it is 200m away. The gradient of the line joining these points is 20, so its average speed for the first 10 seconds is 20m/s.

Note three things:
- At the start it will be going less than 20m/s, at the end it will be going more.
- This information could have been worked out from a table – the graph is not *necessary* to work out average gradients.
- We could work out an average gradient between *any* two points.

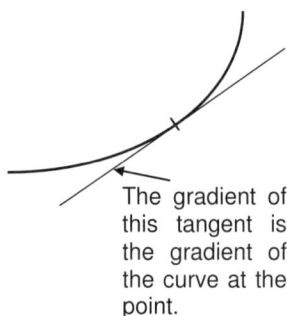

Gradient at a point on a curve: In the example above we calculated the average speed of the car between two times, but we know that the speedo on the car will register the actual speed at a single moment. This is equivalent to the gradient of the curve at a single point. The gradient can be calculated by drawing a *tangent* to the curve and calculating the gradient of the tangent.

The gradient of this tangent is the gradient of the curve at the point.

Special points: You should know the following special points on curves:

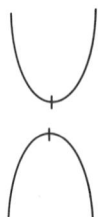

A *minimum*. The gradient is zero. To the left the gradient is <0, to the right it is >0.

A *maximum*. The gradient is zero. To the left the gradient is >0, to the right it is <0.

At each of these points the zero gradient means that the function is momentarily neither increasing or decreasing.

Between the special points: Don't forget that the gradient represents the rate of change of y (ie the function) compared to x.

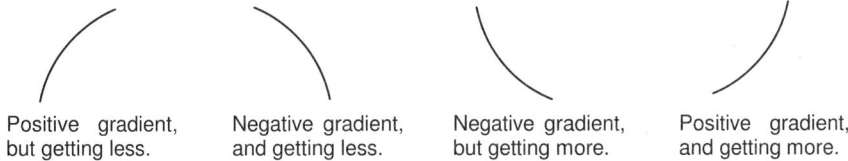

Positive gradient, but getting less.   Negative gradient, and getting less.   Negative gradient, but getting more.   Positive gradient, and getting more.

Calculating the gradient at a point:
Suppose we want to find the gradient of $y = x^2$ at the point (3,9).

The diagram on the right shows part of the curve and the grey, dotted line is the *tangent* at (3,9). The gradient of this line will be the gradient of the curve at the point. Imagine the black dot sliding down the curve: we can calculate the average gradient from (3, 9) to the dot as it passes various points.

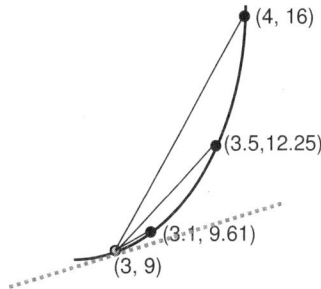

(3,9) → (4,16)   Ave. Grad. = 7
(3,9) → (3.5,12.25)   Ave. Grad. = 6.5
(3,9) → (3.1,9.61)   Ave. Grad. = 6.1

And as we slide down, the average gradients get closer and closer to the gradient at the point. We can guess that it will be about 6, but we can use a formula to confirm this value.

The formula for gradient at a point: By generalising the process of the last section, we can find the gradient at a point (x, y) on the curve of $y = f(x)$ by using the formula:

$$\text{Gradient} = \lim_{h \to 0}\left(\frac{f(x+h) - f(x)}{h}\right)$$

- h is a small distance in the x direction
- "lim" stands for limit: we want to know what the value of the formula is as h gets ever closer to 0

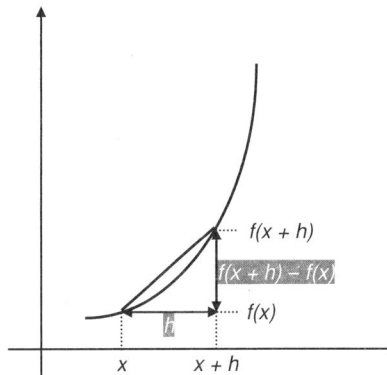

In our example above, $f(x) = x^2$ and $x = 3$.
So the gradient at $x = 3$ can be calculated as:

$$\lim_{h \to 0}\left(\frac{(3+h)^2 - 3^2}{h}\right) = \lim_{h \to 0}\left(\frac{9 + 6h + h^2 - 3^2}{h}\right) = \lim_{h \to 0}\left(\frac{6h + h^2}{h}\right) = \lim_{h \to 0}(6 + h)$$

As h gets close to 0, the limit of this formula is 6: this is the gradient at $x = 3$.

Although you will not be expected to use the formal idea of limits in the exam, you should understand the general principle that the average gradient between two points on a curve gets closer and closer to the gradient at the lower point as the upper one slides towards it (or, of course, the other way around). For example, you may be asked to explain what the formula gives you in a certain situation, and the answer will be "the gradient at the point."

Differentiation

If we had to go through the above calculation every time we wanted a gradient it would be very time consuming. Fortunately, the gradients of functions form distinct rules; applying a rule to find the gradient is called *differentiation*.

Differentiation of polynomials: The only functions you need to be able to differentiate are those with terms of the form ax^n, where *n* can be any integer (including negative).

In general, differentiating ax^n gives nax^{n-1}; in other words, "multiply in front by the power and reduce the power by 1." Note in particular that a term such as $6x$ becomes 6 when differentiated, and a constant (such as 3) becomes 0.

The function you get when you differentiate is called the *derived function* or the *derivative*; think of it as the *gradient function* because it enables you to work out the gradient at any point. The notation used for the derived function is $\frac{dy}{dx}$ or $f'(x)$ (not to be confused with $f^{-1}(x)$ for the inverse function). Some examples of derived functions are:

The function may be expressed using letters other than *x* and *y*. For example, if $h = 2t - 10t^2$ then the notation would be either $f'(t)$ or $\frac{dh}{dt}$.

$f(x)$	$f'(x)$
$3x^2 - 4x + 1$	$6x - 4$
$\frac{1}{3}x^3 - 2x$	$x^2 - 2$
$(x-1)(x-3) = x^2 - 4x + 3$	$2x - 4$
$\frac{2}{x^2} = 2x^{-2}$	$-4x^{-3} = \frac{-4}{x^3}$

Calculating the gradient at a point: The procedure is:
- Differentiate the function
- Substitute the *x*-coordinate into the derived function to get the gradient (note that the *y*-coordinate is irrelevant).

You may also be *given* the gradient at a point and asked to find which point it is. In this case, the procedure is:
- Differentiate the function
- Put the derived function equal to the given gradient
- Solve the equation to find *x*
- Find the *y*-coordinate from the original function (if asked).

For the curve $y = 4x - 2x^3$

i) **Find the gradient at the point (-1, -8)**

If $y = 4x - 2x^3$ then $\frac{dy}{dx} = 4 - 6x^2$. When $x = -1$, $\frac{dy}{dx} = 4 - 6 = \underline{-2}$

ii) **Find the points where the gradient = 2.5**

We need to solve the equation $4 - 6x^2 = 2.5$

$$4 - 6x^2 = 2.5$$
$$1.5 = 6x^2$$
$$x^2 = 0.25$$
$$x = \pm0.5$$

When $x = 0.5$, $y = 4 \times 0.5 - 2 \times (0.5)^3 = 1.75$
When $x = -0.5$, $y = 4 \times (-0.5) - 2 \times (-0.5)^3 = -1.75$

So the gradient is 2.5 at **(0.5, 1.75)** and **(-0.5, -1.75)**

Tangents to Curves

Since differentiation gives us a way to calculate the gradient of a curve at any point, we can extend the calculation to work out the equation of the tangent to a curve at any point. On page 26 you will find the method for finding the equation of a straight line given a point and the gradient. We now have all the tools we need.

The diagram shows a sketch of the graph of $y = x^2 - 4x + 3$.

a) Write down the co-ordinates of the point P where the graph crosses the y axis.

b) Show that the equation of the tangent to the point P is $y + 4x = 3$.

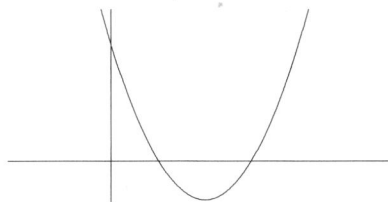

a) When $x = 0$, $y = 0 - 0 + 3$. So the co-ordinates of P are $(0,3)$

b) First we must differentiate the function to find the gradient.

$$y = x^2 - 4x + 3$$

$$\frac{dy}{dx} = 2x - 4$$

So when $x = 0$, $\frac{dy}{dx} = -4$ (Check: the graph is going down at P, so -4 seems OK)

Equation of a straight line is $y - y_1 = m(x - x_1)$
So the equation of the tangent at P is $y - 3 = -4(x - 0)$
$$y - 3 = -4x$$
$$\underline{y + 4x = 3}$$

YOU SOLVE

A curve has equation $y = x^2 - \dfrac{3}{x}$.

a) Find $\dfrac{dy}{dx}$ for this curve.

b) Find the gradient of the curve at the point P where $x = -1$.

c) Show that the tangent to the curve at P has equation $y = x + 5$.

Be very careful with minus signs.

(a) $\underline{2x + 3/x^2}$,　(b) $\underline{1}$

Maximum and Minimum Points

A retailer, for example, may be able to construct a function which relates the profit he makes to the selling price of his product. Too low a price, he doesn't cover his costs; too high a price, it doesn't sell. Somewhere in between he can find the selling price which gives the maximum profit – this will be the turning point on his graph.

Finding the turning points on a graph is particularly useful because such points tell us about the maximum and minimum values of the function. We can find these points by putting the gradient function equal to zero – but which point is which? We can find out by looking at the gradient either side of the turning point. (The procedure is:

- Differentiate the function
- Form an equation by equating the derived function to 0
- Solve the equation to find the x value of the turning point
- Find the y value if required
- Find the gradient either side of the turning point by drawing a *sign diagram*
- From the sign diagram, decide if you have a maximum or a minimum.

The velocity v ms^{-1} of a kite after t secs is given by $v = t^3 - 4t^2 + 4t$.

a)   Find the velocity of the kite after 0.5s and after 1s.

Substitute t = 0.5 into the velocity to get <u>**v = 1.125ms^{-1}**</u>

Substitute t = 1 into the velocity to get <u>**v = 1ms^{-1}**</u>

b)   Find $\dfrac{dv}{dt}$ in terms of t. Find the value of t at the maximum and minimum values of the function.

$\dfrac{dv}{dt} = 3t^2 - 8t + 4$. For a max or min, $\dfrac{dv}{dt} = 0$, so:

$$3t^2 - 8t + 4 = 0$$
$$(3t - 2)(t - 2) = 0$$

So the turning points are at <u>**t = 0.667**</u> and <u>**t = 2**</u>.

The question did not ask us to identify which is the maximum and which the minimum, but the sign diagram is drawn up like this:

- Choose values of t either side of the turning point(s)
- Draw up a table showing these values and the turning point values
- Work out the gradient at each point (you only need to know if it is >0, =0 or <0) by substituting into the derived function
- Identify the nature of the points

t	0	0.667	1	2	3
Gradient	>0 (4)	0	<0 (-1)	0	>0 (7)
	/	—	\	—	/

So at $t = 0.667$ there is a maximum and at $t = 2$ there is a minimum. What do these turning points represent? They show when the velocity is at its greatest or at its least. The graph of the function is:

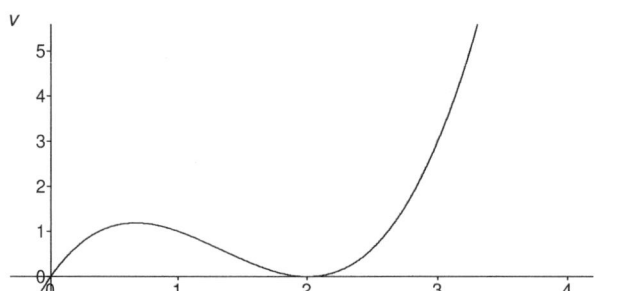

So the kite starts moving at $t = 0$ and accelerates until $t = 0.667$. At this point it slows down (but v is still positive, so it is still going up) until it stops momentarily at $t = 2$, then it speeds up again.

Using your calculator: Your calculator can perform a number of useful calculations when in graphing mode. In particular, make sure you know how to use it to:

- Find the y value at a point
- Find the gradient at a point
- Find where the graph cuts the x-axis
- Find minimum and maximum points.

The last two may give rise to several points (for example, the graph on the previous page cuts the x-axis at two points). The calculator will not know which point you want, so it will always ask you for a *left bound* and a *right bound* before you can find the required point.

A function has equation $y = (x - 1)^3 \, 2^{-x}$.
a)   **Find the coordinates of the point where the graph intercepts the x-axis.**
b)   **Find the coordinates of the maximum point.**
c)   **Find the gradient at the point where $x = 7$. What does the sign of the gradient tell you about the shape of the graph at that point.**
d)   **What is the equation of the tangent at the point where $x = 3$?**
Draw the graph first and spend some time adjusting the window; this will give you a "feel" for the function. For part (d), find the gradient of the tangent and the y value. Use this to find the equation of the tangent. When you have found the equation, draw it, and you can check it really is the tangent.

(a) <u>(1, 0)</u> (b) <u>(5.33, 2.02)</u> (c) <u>-0.326, the graph is descending</u> (d) <u>$y = 0.807x - 1.421$</u>

YOU SOLVE

In summary, remember that when you *differentiate* a function, the resulting function gives you the *gradient* (or *rate of change*) of the original function at any point. This can then be used in a number of ways: for example, finding tangents, calculating maximum and minimum points.

FINANCIAL MATHEMATICS

Basics of Financial Mathematics

Currency conversion: The exchange rate between two currencies is always quoted by comparing 1 unit in one of the currencies with the equivalent amount in the other currency. Use the reciprocal of this rate to work out the rate from the second currency back to the first. eg: $1 = 2.45 crowns. The reciprocal of 2.45 is $\frac{1}{2.45}$ = 0.408 so 1 crown = $0.408. Which rate do you use? If, for example, you are asked to convert $62 to crowns, say to yourself: $1 is 2.45 crowns, so $62 is 62 × 2.45 crowns. And the answer is therefore 151.90 crowns.

When working out currency calculations, give 2dp accuracy

Commission: Agencies which exchange currency make their money on the deal by making a charge (the commission).The commission rate is often subject to a minimum charge. For example: "Commission is 1.5% or $5, whichever is greater." Using the rates quoted above, how many crowns would we get for $50 and for $500?

- **$50**. 1.5% of $50 is $0.75, so $5 will be charged. We therefore only have $45 to exchange, and this will give us 45 × 2.45 = 110.25 crowns.
- **$500**. 1.5% of $500 is $7.50, so this is the amount charged. We only have $492.50 to exchange, and this will give us 492.5 × 2.45 = 1206.63 crowns.

Spread: Another way of making a profit is to charge different amounts for buying and selling. For example, the quoted rates may be: "We will sell you crowns at $1 = 2.42 crowns and we will buy crowns from you at $1 = 2.48 crowns. To see how this works:

- $1000 can be changed into 1000 × 2.42 = 2420 crowns.
- 2420 crowns can be changed into 2420 ÷ 2.48 = $975.81.

Thus the profit on the deal is $24.19, equivalent to about 2.4%.

Simple and Compound Interest: These topics are discussed on page 10. There are two formulae which can be used, but it is often easier to calculate from basic principles.

I = amount of interest paid
C = the amount of the loan or investment (the "capital")
R = the interest rate (as a percentage)
N = the number of time periods

SIMPLE INTEREST FORMULA	COMPOUND INTEREST FORMULA
$I = \dfrac{CRN}{100}$	$I = C\left(1 + \dfrac{R}{100}\right)^N - C$

If you use the compound interest formula, it is important to realise that the amount in the account is $C\left(1 + \dfrac{R}{100}\right)^N$. Subtracting C, the original amount, tells us how much interest has been paid overall. As with all formulae, a question may ask you to calculate the value of a letter other than the one on the left hand side (the amount of interest).

£1000 is invested at an interest rate of 6% per annum compounded yearly.
a)   What is the amount after 3 years?
b)   How many months will £1000 take to increase to £1100 if invested at an interest rate of 6% per annum compounded monthly?

a)   Using the formula, the amount after 3 years is $1000 \times 1.06^3 = $ __£1191.02__
Remember that to increase by 6% you multiply by 1.06. This is reflected in the formula in the term $1 + \dfrac{R}{100}$.

b)   When compounded monthly this is the same as increasing the investment by 0.5% per month. (This is *more* than 6% per year because each 0.5% increase applies to a slightly larger amount as the year progresses). So we need to solve the equation $1000 \times 1.005^N = 1100$; in other words, how many times do we increase by 0.5% before we get £1100?

To solve this, use trial and error on your calculator. You will find that you must carry out 20 increases to double your money, so the answer is __20 months.__

The following is an example of a more general financial question.

When selling a house, an agent receives 2% on the first £30 000 and 1.5% on the remainder of the price of the house as commission.
a)   How much does he receive when selling a house for £330 000?
        2% of 30 000 = 0.02 × 30 000 = £600
There is now £300 000 left, and this will earn commission at 1.5%.
        1.5% of 300 000 = 0.015 × 300 000 = £4500
        Total commission = 600 + 4500 = __£5100__
b)   What is the selling price of the house if the agent receives £1650 as commission?
The first bit of the commission will *always* be 2% of 30 000 = £600.
In this case, this leaves £1050 to go. So the question is: "1050 is 1.5% of what?" Two ways of doing this. Play around on the calculator (ie trial and error) until you get the right answer. Or form an equation (replacing "what" with x).
        1.5% of x = 1050
        $0.015 \times x = 1050$
        $x = 1050/0.015 = 70\ 000$
Remember that this is the value of the house *above* £30 000. So the price of the house is 30 000 + 70 000 = __£100 000__
(In this sort of question, it's always worth checking the answer by working forwards as in part (a))

The table shows part of a currency conversion chart. For example GBP 1 is equivalent to $AUS 2.33.

	GBP	$US	$AUS
GBP	1	s	2.33
$US	0.571	1	t
$AUS	0.429	0.751	1

Giving answers correct to 2 decimal places:
a)   Calculate the values of s and t.
        (Remember the reciprocal rule)

b)   Joe has $US 2500 to exchange at a bank.
        i)   If no commission is charged, how much will Joe receive in GBP?
        ii)   Assuming the bank charges 1.3% commission:
                a)   How much in GBP does Joe pay in commission?
                b)   How much in GBP does Joe actually receive for his USD 2500?

        a) $s = 1.75$, $t = 1.33$ b) (i) __GBP 1427.50__   (ii)(a) __GBP 18.56__   (ii)(b) __GBP 1408.94__

Tables and Schemes

Financial tables: Tables are often used to give information about investments or loan repayments which enable interest amounts to be calculated without using the formulae. For example, a table may show the monthly repayments for a £10000 loan using various interest rates and repayment periods. Part of the table would look like this:

Years to repay	at 3%	at 5%	at 8%
1	846.94	856.07	869.88
2	429.81	438.71	452.27
3	290.81	299.71	313.36
4	221.34	230.29	244.13
5	179.69	188.71	202.76

So if you were to repay at 5% over a 2 year period, you would be repaying at £438.71/month. 2 years is 24 months, so your total repayment would be $24 \times 438.71 = £10529.04$. Note that:

- The longer the time period, the more interest you pay and therefore the more expensive the loan is.
- Repayment amounts are not proportional eg doubling the repayment period does not double the amount you pay, nor does doubling the interest rate.

Schemes: A question may involve certain schemes for investment, loan repayment, salary increases and so on, and you will probably be asked to compare different schemes. The maths you need to use could involve anything discussed so far eg percentages, simple or compound interest, tables and so on.

Angela needs $4000 to pay for a car. She was given two options by the car seller.

OPTION A: *Outright Loan*
A loan of $4000 at a rate of 12% compounded monthly.
a)   Find the cost of this loan for one year and the equivalent annual simple interest rate.
Amount = $4000, interest rate = 1%, no. of time periods = 12.
So, amount to pay = 4000×1.01^{12} = $4507.30. But the question asks for the *cost* of the loan, ie how much interest has been paid. This is $4507.30 - 4000 =$ **$507.30**

We need this number as a % of 4000. Equivalent simple interest rate = $\dfrac{507.30}{4000} \times 100 =$ **12.7%**

OPTION B: *Friendly credit terms*
A 25% deposit followed by 12 equal monthly payments of £287.50.
b)   How much is to be paid as a deposit, and how much does the loan cost?
The deposit is 25% of 4000 = $0.25 \times 4000 =$ **$1000**
12 payments of 287.50 make $3450, so the total cost is $1000 + 3450 =$ $4450, so the cost of the loan is **$450**.

c)   Give a reason why Angela might choose Option A and a reason why she might choose option B.
Option B is cheaper overall, but she may not be able to pay the high deposit. In other words, Option A spreads the payments out better.

To help Angela, her employer agrees to lend her $4000 interest free. He will then make deductions from her salary amounting to $x in the first month and $y every subsequent month. After 20 months he has deducted $1540 and after 30 months $2140.
d)   Find x and y, and work out how many months it will take Angela to pay off the loan.
When you are asked to "find x and y" this usually means simultaneous equations. After 20 months the deductions will amount to $x + 19y$ and after 30 months $x + 29y$. So:

$$\left. \begin{array}{l} x + 19y = 1540 \\ x + 29y = 2140 \end{array} \right\} \Rightarrow 10y = 600 . \text{ So } \underline{y = \$60} \text{ and } \underline{x = \$400}$$

To find when the loan is paid off, find out how many times you add 60 to 400 to reach 4000. (This can be done by equation or trial and error). You need 60 additions, so the total number of months is **61**.

© IBO Nov 99

ASSESSMENT DETAILS

The two Studies papers count for 80% of your final mark, the remaining 20% being contributed by the internally assessed portfolio.

You should prepare yourself carefully for the exams, allowing for all eventualities. For example, make sure you have a spare set of batteries for your GDC, and that it only has legal programs in its memory. You should take at least two pens, and also pencils, ruler and eraser for drawing diagrams. You will be given a clean copy of the information booklet (you cannot take your own in); if you have not used it very much during lessons, part of your revision should involve getting to know the booklet well so that you can easily find relevant formulae and tables.

Paper 1 consists of 15 short response questions. Since the paper is 90 minutes long, you should be aiming to answer one question every 5 minutes, allowing 15 minutes for a good check at the end. However, remember that the questions are set at varying levels of difficulty, so the 5 minutes is very much a mean time – aim for at least 1 mark per minute. Show enough working so that you can still gain method marks even if the answer is wrong.

Paper 2 consists of 5 extended response questions. To ensure a reasonable coverage of the syllabus, some questions may consist of unconnected parts, and will be clearly shown as such. Where a question has connected parts, make sure you use what you have worked out in the earlier parts to answer the later parts. Sometimes, too, you may find a clue in a later part which helps you to answer an earlier part. Generally, the questions will start quite easily and will become relatively harder. It is crucial that you show full working and clear reasoning in this paper. Again, the paper is 90 minutes and, again, try and make sure you are working faster than 1 mark per minute.

Each of papers 1 and 2 require full knowledge of the core syllabus and each is worth 40% of the final total.

▦ A reminder that you must *not* use calculator notation in exam questions. If you write LinReg(ax + b) instead of showing appropriate working with mathematical notation, you could well lose marks – and if the answer is wrong you will gain no method marks. Similarly, if you calculate a definite integral on your GDC, make sure you write down the integral correctly as your working; calculator notation such as fnInt is unacceptable.

PRACTICE QUESTIONS

The questions which follow are not designed to cover every aspect of the syllabus, nor are they exam style questions. Their purpose is to give you some practice in the *basics*: if you cannot, for example, carry out a straightforward differentiation, then you will get questions which depend on accurate differentiation wrong, even if you know exactly how to do the question. So you need to answer all these questions as part of your revision. If you get an answer wrong, find out why: then come back to it later, and see if you can get it right next time.

NUMBER AND ALGEBRA

1. Calculate $\dfrac{4.523}{6.81 \times 2.47}$ giving your answer to 3 SF.

2. A triangle has a base of 12.5 cm and a height of 7.8 cm, both measurements to 1 D.P. What is the maximum possible area?

3. What is the percentage error if the fraction $\frac{22}{7}$ is used for π?

4. If a computer carries out 5.6×10^9 calculations per second, how long does 1 calculation take. Give your answer in standard form.

5. Convert 58 km/h into m/s.

6. Find the 25th term and the sum of the first 54 terms of the sequence which begins: 3, 8, 13, 18 …

7. An arithmetic sequence has first term 7 and common difference 3.5. How many terms are required for the sum of the sequence to be 25830.

8. What is the 12th term and the sum to 18 terms of the sequence which begins 3, 12, 48, 192?

9. A geometric series has a first term 400, ten terms and a sum of 1295.67. What is the common ratio?

10. How much will an investment of $6300 be worth (to the nearest dollar) after accumulating compound interest for 12 years at a rate of 3% per annum? If 1.5% interest is paid every 6 months, how much will the investment be worth after 12 years?

11. Find the solution of the simultaneous equations $2y = 3x + 5$ and $6x + 3y = 11$ using both an algebraic and a calculator method.

12. Rearrange the equation $3x^2 + 5x = x^2 - 2$ so that the right hand side equals 0. Solve the equation using by a calculator method.

13. Factorise $x^2 + 7x - 60$ and hence solve the equation $x^2 + 7x - 60 = 0$.

SETS, LOGIC AND PROBABILITY

1. List the members of the following three sets:

    $A = \{x \mid x \text{ is even}, 2 \le x < 8\}$; $B = \{x \mid x \in \mathbb{Z}, 1 \le x \le 5\}$; $A \cap B$

2. If $C = \{\text{all even numbers}\}$, and A and B are defined as in the previous question, which of the following are true: $A \subset C$; $C \subset A$; $A = C$; $B \cap C = \varnothing$; $A \cap C' = \varnothing$

3. Make copies of the Venn Diagram on the right and shade areas to represent: $P \cap Q$; $P' \cap Q$; $P' \cup Q'$; $(P' \cup Q)'$

4. Make a copy of the Venn Diagram and add another set R such that $R \subset P$ and $R \cap Q = \varnothing$.

5. Make a copy of the Venn Diagram and fill in the number of elements in each region such that: $n(U) = 30$, $n(P) = 18$; $n(Q) = 6$; $n(P \cup Q) = 21$.

6. Draw a four row truth table and complete columns for the following propositions: $p \Rightarrow q$; $\neg p \wedge q$; $p \vee (p \wedge \neg q)$; $\neg(p \veebar q)$.

7. Show that the proposition $p \Rightarrow (p \vee q)$ is a tautology.

8. On an eight row truth table, complete a column for the proposition $(\neg p \vee q) \Rightarrow r$.

9. "If it is hot we will go to the beach." Write down the converse, the inverse and the contrapositive statements.

10. Two dice are thrown. What is P(at least one shows a number greater than 1)?

11. I have 6 red socks and 4 green socks in a draw. I take 2 out at random. Draw a tree diagram to show the possible outcomes and find P(the two socks do not match).

12. A and B are two events such that P(A) = 0.2, P(B) = 0.5 and P(A ∪ B) = 0.55. Use a Venn Diagram to find: P(A ∩ B); P(A' ∩ B); P(A|B); P(B|A).

13. Two dice are rolled. Find the probability that they show different numbers given that the total is 8.

14. Given that P(A ∪ B) = 0.7, P(A) = 0.6 and that A and B are independent events, find P(B).

FUNCTIONS

1. What is the range of the function $f : x \rightarrow x^2 + 2$, $x \geq 1$?
2. Sketch the graph of $f : x \rightarrow \sqrt{(2 - x)}$, and hence write down the domain and range of the function.
3. Write down the gradients, x and y intercepts of the following straight line functions: $y = 2x - 5$; $3x - 2y = 8$; $x + y = 10$
4. Work out the equation of the line perpendicular to $y = 3x - 4$, which goes through the point (1, 1).
5. Find the line of symmetry and the vertex of the graph of $y = x^2 - 2x + 6$.
6. For the graph of $y = 2(x - 3)(x + 1)$, write down the coordinates of the x intercepts, the y intercept and the vertex.
7. Some radioactive material decays such that its mass after t years is given by the formula $m = 12 \times 2^{-0.008t}$. What is its mass at $t = 0$ and after 100 years?
8. The graph with equation $y = 3^{2x} + k$ passes through the point (1, 6). Find the value of k and find x when $y = -2$.
9. Write down the amplitude and period of the following functions: $f(x) = 2\sin x$; $f(x) = \sin 3x$; $f(x) = 2\cos 10x + 3$.
10. At a certain location the height of the tide is given by $h = 5 + 3\sin 30t$ where h is in metres and t in hours after noon. Find the height of the tide at 16:30, and also the first two times after noon when the height is 3m.
11. Use your GDC to solve the following equations: $x + 3 = \dfrac{2}{x}$; $x^3 = 2^x$.
12. Find the horizontal and vertical asymptotes on the graph of $y = \dfrac{2 + x}{3 - x}$.
13. Sketch the graph of the function $f(x) = \dfrac{x}{30}\sin x°$ for $0° \leq x \leq 360°$, marking the coordinates of all intercepts and turning points.

GEOMETRY AND TRIGONOMETRY

1. For the points A(2,3) and B(4,7), find: the midpoint; the distance AB; the gradient of AB; the equation of AB.
2. Repeat question 1 for the points A(-1,4) and B(-3,7).
3. Write down which pairs of lines are parallel and which are perpendicular:
   (a) $y = 2x + 5$; (b) $y + 2x = 1$; (c) $x = 4$; (d) $2y = x$; (e) $y - 2x + 3 = 0$; (f) $y = 3$.
4. Triangle PQR has a right angle at Q. PQ = 12cm, R = 23°. Calculate PR.
5. Triangle ABC has a right angle at A. AC = 2.4cm, AB = 1.8cm. Find C.
6. Solve the following triangles (the triangle in each case is ABC):
   BC = 6cm, C = 87°, A = 45°. Find AB.
   AB = 6cm, A = 87°, AC = 5.4cm. Find BC.
   AB = 6cm, BC = 5.4cm, CA = 3.5cm. Find B.
   AB = BC = 5.2cm. B = 34°. Find AC.
   AC = 6cm, C = 32°, A = 90°. Find AB.
   BC = 6cm, B = 62°, C = 71°. Find AC.
7. Find the area of the first and second triangles in question 6.

8. A line AB of length 60m is marked out on a river bank and the position of a tree C on the opposite bank is surveyed. It is found that CAB = 58° and CBA = 38°. Find CA and the width of the river.

9. Calculate the volume and surface area of a sealed cylinder with radius 3.5cm and height 8.3cm.

10. Calculate the volume and surface area of a sphere with diameter 8m.

11. Calculate the radius of a sphere with volume $128cm^3$.

12. Calculate the curved surface area of a cone with radius 5cm and height 8cm.

13. The square based pyramid on the right has AB = 10cm and
AE = 12cm. Q is the midpoint of AB. Calculate the following:
The lengths AC, AP, PE, QE.
The angle between AE and the base.
The angle between QE and the base.
The angle between EB and EC.
The surface area of the pyramid (including the base).

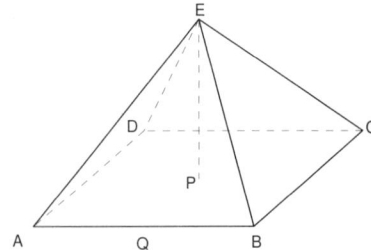

STATISTICS

15.60	5.95	31.22	3.02	6.60	24.70	15.45	32.50	12.45	4.43
12.65	10.09	52.86	12.88	2.53	31.79	9.86	25.79	18.28	32.05
14.87	24.65	15.70	8.65	4.42	17.20	8.53	0.45	0.95	4.44
7.45	5.82	45.20	2.70	10.04	15.70	32.20	12.43	36.75	32.50
16.87	3.78	0.56	33.67	9.67	25.50	33.06	7.56	2.63	45.80

The amount spent (in €) by the first 50 people going into a shop is shown in the table above. Questions 1 to 9 refer to this table.

1. Is this data discrete or continuous?
2. Draw up a grouped frequency table (with first group €0.01 – €10.00). You should have 6 groups.
3. Which is the modal group?
4. Enter the mid-values of each group and the frequencies onto your GDC. Calculate estimates of the mean and the standard deviation. (Why "estimates")?
5. Draw a bar chart to represent the data.
6. Complete a cumulative frequency table for the data, and hence draw a cumulative frequency graph.
7. From the cumulative frequency graph, write down the median, the lower quartile, the upper quartile and calculate the interquartile range.
8. Draw a box and whisker plot for the data.
9. What was the least amount that the people in the top ten percentiles spent?
10.

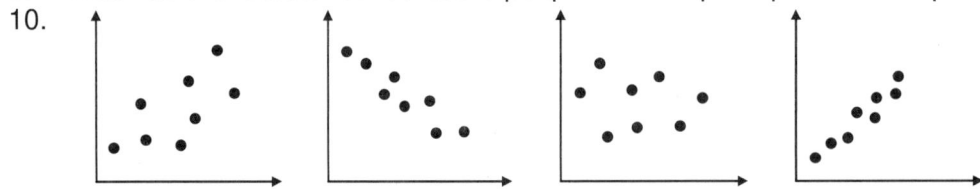

Match each of the scattergraphs above with one of the correlation coefficients
-0.85, 0.0, 0.64, 0.92.

11. The table below shows the marks gained by 12 students in a chemistry assignments and a chemistry test.

Assignment (x)	5	9	7	11	20	4	6	17	12	10	15	16
Test (y)	6	8	9	13	20	9	8	17	14	8	17	18

Calculate the correlation coefficient, and find the regression line $y = ax + b$.

12. A thirteenth pupil missed the test because of illness. If she got 18 in the assignment, what mark should she be given in the test?

13. A set of 7 pairs (x,y) of data has $\Sigma x = 91$, $\Sigma y = 165$, $s_x = 5.73$, $s_y = 2.44$, $s_{xy} = 6.567$. Calculate the correlation coefficient and the regression line $y = ax + b$.

14. A random sample of 100 people were asked whether or not they drank "X-Lite". 62 said yes and 38 said no. After an advertising campaign another sample of 80 was asked the same question. 56 said yes and 24 said no. Draw up contingency tables

for the observed and expected frequencies (Columns: Yes/No; Rows: Before/After campaign). Carry out a test at the 5% level to see if the advertising campaign has had an effect.

INTRODUCTORY DIFFERENTIAL CALCULUS

1. Differentiate the following functions:

$$f(x) = 2x^3 - 3x^2 + 4x - 3; \quad f(x) = x + \frac{6}{x}; \quad f(x) = 4 - \frac{2}{x^3}$$

2. What is the gradient of each of the curves in question 1 at the point where $x = 2$?
3. Find the equation of the tangent to $y = 3x^2 + 3$ at the point where $x = 1$.
4. Find the two points on the graph of $y = x - \frac{2}{x}$ where the gradient = 3.
5. By finding the values of $f(x)$ and $f'(x)$ at the points where $x = 2$ and $x = 3$ on the graph of $y = \frac{1}{2}x^2 - 2x + 1$, sketch the shape of the graph between the two points.
6. Use differentiation to find the turning point on the graph of $y = 6 - x + 3x^2$.
7. Use differentiation to find both turning points on the graph of $2x^3 - 24x$. Draw a sign diagram to decide which point is a maximum and which is a minimum.
8. Use your calculator to find all the turning points on the graph of $f(x) = x^2 \times 2^x$. State which are maxima and which are minima. Give answers to 3 significant figures where appropriate.
9. Find the gradient of the line joining the points (2, 6) and (3, 11) on the graph of $y = x^2 + 2$. Repeat for the line joining the points with x-coordinates 2 and 2.5, and then the line joining points with x-coordinates 2 and 2.1. What do your results suggest about the gradient of the tangent to the graph at the point where $x = 2$?

FINANCIAL MATHEMATICS

1. If £3.50 = €5.39, convert £1 to €, and €1 to £.
2. If $1 = 12.8 crowns, how many dollars would 150 crowns be worth?
3. A bank charges commission when converting currency as follows: the charge is 5% or $3.50, whichever is larger. Using the conversion rate in question 2, how many crowns would a customer receive when changing $50? And how many crowns for $500.
4. I invest $2500 at 3% compound interest. How much will my investment be worth in 10 years? What would be the equivalent rate of simple interest?
5. How many years will it take for an investment of £1500 to grow to £2500 at a rate of 6%, compounded annually?
6. I buy a car for €9000 and it depreciates at 30% per year for two years and then at 20% per year for another 3 years. How much will it then be worth, to the nearest euro?
7. How much more would a £5200 investment be worth after 4 years if the compound interest rate is 0.5% per month instead of 6% per year?
8. Set up a table on your GDC which shows the annual value of a $200 investment growing at 4% compound interest per year. Use your table to write down after how many years the investment will be worth more than $300 and after how many years it will have trebled in value.
9. If my house has increased in value by 2.5% in the last year, and it is now worth €150,000, what was it worth one year ago?
10. Use the table on page 60 to work out how much in total you would pay if you were to take out a $20000 loan at 8% over 4 years.
11. I put $AUS2000 into a savings account at the start of *each* year for 5 years. The total investment gains 4% per year. What is it worth at the end of the 5 years?

Answers to Practice Questions

NUMBER AND ALGEBRA
1. 0.269   **2.** 49.25875cm^2 **3.** 0.040%   **4.** 1.79×10^{-10} **5.** 16.11 m/s
6. 123, 7317   **7.** 120   **8.** 12582912, 6.87×10^{10} **9.** 0.7   **10.** \$8982, \$9006
11. $x = 1/3$, $y = 3$ **12.** $2x^2 + 5x + 2 = 0$, -0.5 or -0.2   **13.** $(x-5)(x+12)$, 5 or -12

SETS, LOGIC AND PROBABILITY
1. {2,3,4,5,6,7}, {1,2,3,4,5}, {2,3,4,5}   **2.** T,F,F,F,T
3.

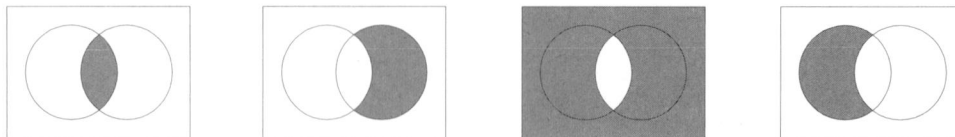

4.

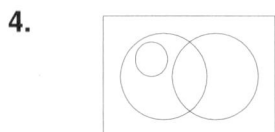

5.

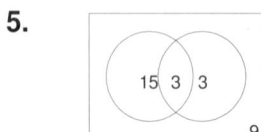

15 3 3

9

7.

P	q	$p \vee q$	$p \Rightarrow (p \vee q)$
T	T	T	T
T	F	T	T
F	T	T	T
F	F	F	T

Tautology

6.

P	q	$p \Rightarrow q$	$\neg p \wedge q$	$p \vee \neg q$	$\neg(p \underline{\vee} q)$
T	T	T	F	T	T
T	F	F	F	T	F
F	T	T	T	F	F
F	F	T	F	T	T

8.

p	q	r	$\neg p$	$\neg p \vee q$	$\neg p \vee q \Rightarrow r$
T	T	T	F	T	T
T	T	F	F	T	F
T	F	T	F	F	T
T	F	F	F	F	T
F	T	T	T	T	T
F	T	F	T	T	F
F	F	T	T	T	T
F	F	F	T	T	F

9. "If we go to the beach it is hot."
"If it isn't hot, we won't go to the beach."
"If we don't go to the beach, it isn't hot."

10. 35/36

11.

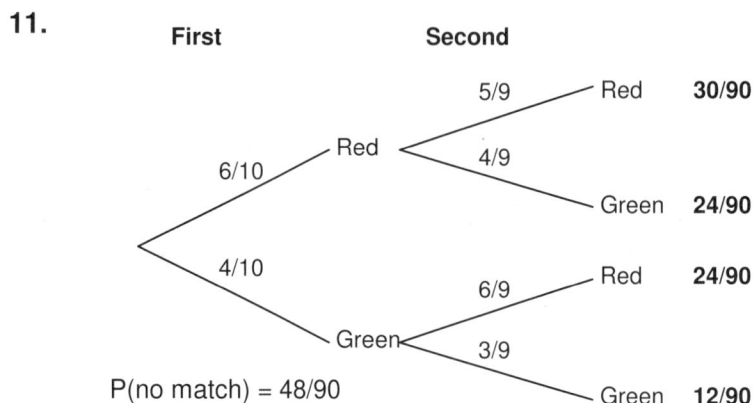

First   Second

6/10 Red   5/9 Red   **30/90**
              4/9 Green **24/90**
4/10 Green 6/9 Red   **24/90**
              3/9 Green **12/90**

P(no match) = 48/90

12.

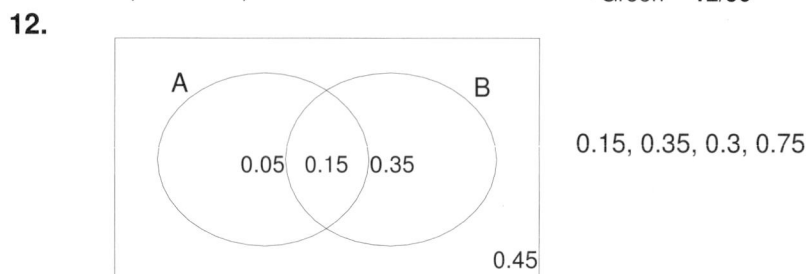

A   B
0.05 0.15 0.35

0.45

0.15, 0.35, 0.3, 0.75

13. 4/5   **14.** 0.25

FUNCTIONS

1. $f(x) \geq 3$ **2.** 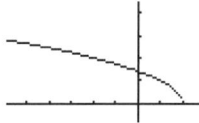 $x \leq 2$, $f(x) \geq 0$ **3.** 2, 2.5, -5; 1.5,8/3, -4; -1, 10, 10

4. $x + 3y = 4$ **5.** $x = 1$, (1,5) **6.** (3,0), (-1,0); (0,-6); (1,-8) **7.** 12, 6.89 **8.** −3, 0
9. 2, 360º; 1, 120º; 2, 36º **10.** 7.12m, 19:24 and 20:36 **11.** 0.562 and −3.56, 1.373
12. $y = -1$, $x = 3$ **13.**

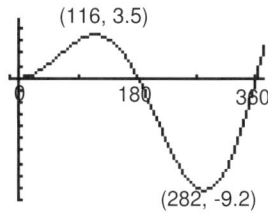

GEOMETRY AND TRIGONOMETRY

1. (3,5), 4.47, 2, $y = 2x - 1$. **2.** (-2,5.5), 3.61, -1.5, $2y + 3x = 5$ **3.** ‖ a,e. ⊥ c,f; b,d.
4. 30.7 **5.** 36.9º **6.** 8.47, 7.86, 35.3º, 3.04, 3.75, 7.24 **7.** 18.9, 16.2 **8.** 37.1, 31.5
9. $319.4cm^3$, $259.5cm^2$ **10.** $268.1m^3$, $201.1m^2$ **11.** 3.13cm **12.** $148.2cm^2$
13. 14.1cm, 7.07cm, 9.70cm, 10.9cm; 53.9º; 62.7º; 49.2º; $318cm^2$

STATISTICS

1. Discrete. **2.**

0.01 – 10.00	10.01 – 20.00	20.01 – 30.00	30.01 – 40.00	40.01 – 50.00	50.01 – 60.00
20	14	5	8	2	1

3. 0.01 – 10.00 **4.** 17.2, 13.31; not using original data.
5.

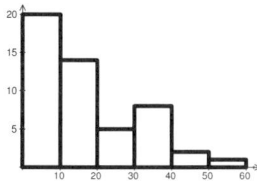

6.

€	≤10	≤ 20	≤ 30	≤ 40	≤ 50	≤60
c.f.	20	34	39	47	49	50

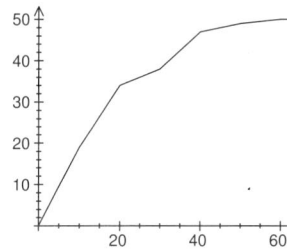

8.

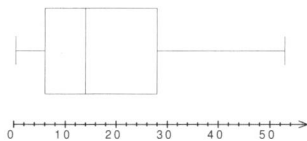

7. $Q_1 = 6$, $Q_2 = 14$, $Q_3 = 28$, IQR = 22

9. €38 **10.** 0.64, -0.85, 0.0, 0.92 **11.** 0.94, $y = 0.88x + 2.58$ **12.** 18.4
13. 0.47, $y = 0.2x + 21$ **14.** $\chi^2 = 1.26$, c.v. = 3.841. Campaign ineffective.

INTRODUCTORY DIFFERENTIAL CALCULUS

1. $6x^2 - 6x + 4$, $1 - \dfrac{6}{x^2}$, $\dfrac{6}{x^4}$. **2.** 16, -0.5, 0.375 **3.** $y = 6x$ **4.** (1,-1), (-1,1)

5. $f(x) = -1$ and -0.5, $f'(x) = 0$ and 1 **6.** $\left(\frac{1}{6}, 5\frac{11}{12}\right)$ **7.** (2,-32) min, (-2,32) max

8. (-2.89, 1.13) max, (0,0) min **9.** 5, 4.5, 4.1; Tending towards 4.

FINANCIAL MATHEMATICS

1. €1.54, £0.65 **2.** $11.72 **3.** 684.8 crowns, 6720 crowns **4.** $3359.80, 3.44%
5. 9 years **6.** €2258 **7.** $41.66 **8.** 11 years, 29 years **9.** €146341.46
10. $23436.48 **11.** $AUS11265.95

Version 2.16